The Separation of the Methodists from the Church of England

BY
ROBERT LEONARD TUCKER, M.A.

SUBMITTED IN PARTIAL FULFILLMENT OF THE
REQUIREMENTS FOR THE
DEGREE OF DOCTOR OF PHILOSOPHY
COLUMBIA UNIVERSITY

WIPF & STOCK · Eugene, Oregon

Wipf and Stock Publishers
199 W 8th Ave, Suite 3
Eugene, OR 97401

The Separation of the Methodists from the Church of England
By Tucker, Robert Leonard
ISBN 13: 978-1-60608-302-4
Publication date 10/24/2008
Previously published by The Methodist Book Concern, 1918

TO
MY WIFE
GRACE GREEN TUCKER
MY MOTHER
FANNIE ALLUM TUCKER
MY FATHER
JOHN TUCKER
THREE METHODISTS WHOSE LIVES SHOW THAT NOBLEST SPIRIT OF TRUE RELIGION FAR MORE CLEARLY THAN ALL MY WORDS, THIS TASK IS DEDICATED

CONTENTS

	PAGE
PREFACE	7
INTRODUCTION	9
CHAPTER I. THE METHODIST VIEW OF EIGHTEENTH CENTURY LIFE	11
I. Methodist Dissatisfaction with the Customs and Religion of the Times	11
II. Methodist View of the Church and the Clergy	12
CHAPTER II. THE CHURCHMAN'S VIEW OF EIGHTEENTH CENTURY LIFE	17
I. Enthusiasm	17
II. The Church View of Enthusiasm	23
III. Methodist Attempts to Check Extreme Enthusiasm	30
IV. Methodism and Mysticism	34
CHAPTER III. METHODIST DOCTRINE	37
I. Original Sin	37
II. Justification by Faith	39
III. The New Birth	42
IV. Christian Perfection	48
V. The Witness of the Spirit	53
VI. The Early Methodist Doctrine of the Church	55
VII. The Orthodoxy of Early Methodist Doctrine	57
CHAPTER IV. PRACTICES OF THE EARLY METHODISTS	62
I. Early Field Preaching	63
II. Early Irregular Indoor Preaching	70
III. The Beginning of the Itinerancy	71
IV. The Use of Lay Preachers	74
V. The First Methodist Ordinations	83
CHAPTER V. THE GROWTH OF THE EARLY METHODIST ORGANIZATION	96
I. Methodist Societies	96
II. The Beginning of the Methodist Conferences	104
III. Methodist Classes, Bands, Stewards, Quarterly Meetings	111
IV. The Methodist Press	117
V. Summary	123
CHAPTER VI. DEVELOPMENT OF METHODIST SOLIDARITY	125
I. Wesley's Opposition to the Unification of Methodism	125
II. Bishops of the Established Church and Methodism	130
III. Confusion of Methodists with Catholics	136
IV. Opposition to the Methodists	138
CHAPTER VII. THE ACTUAL SEPARATION AFTER THE DEATH OF WESLEY	144
I. Paternal Government	144
II. The Eucharist	145
III. Hours of Church Service	149
IV. The Confusion after Wesley's Death	153
V. Party Struggle and the Sacrament	156
VI. Trusteeism and the Methodist New Connection	161
VII. Plan of Pacification and Regulations of Leeds	166
CONCLUSION	171
BIBLIOGRAPHY	175

PREFACE

THIS work is undertaken with the conviction that the profoundest interpretation of the Methodist movement must ultimately be sociological. History may give us the facts; but one must turn to sociology for any satisfying explanation of those facts.

At the beginning of the Methodist movement, the Churchmen and the majority of the Methodists were members of the same sociological "group". There were many causes contributing toward the breaking up of this group, and not least among these was the difference in emphasis on doctrine, as well as the efficient and highly centralized organization built up by Wesley and his followers. Opposition to the organization served only to strengthen the movement. Conscious of an ever-increasing strength, and opposed on every hand, the Methodists took a series of steps: they ordained their preachers without permission from the Church; they refused to take the sacrament from the clergy, but administered it in their preaching houses; in Church hours they conducted divine worship; they registered their meeting houses as places of dissent. These steps completed the separation. The so-called *Plan of Pacification* and the *Regulations of Leeds* consciously and explicitly confirmed the break. The purpose of this work is to trace the factors resulting in disrupting the sociological group, and thereby making the separation of the Methodists from the Church of England a historical fact.

The works here used are listed in the bibliography at the back of the book; but it is necessary to explain the use of the following books: 1. All references in the footnotes to the *Journal* refer to *John Wesley's Journal,* published in eight volumes by Eaton and Mains, New York, 1909, under the editorship of the Rev. Nehemiah Curnock. This edition is the latest and most scholarly; and is especially rich in notes and documents not readily found elsewhere. 2. All references to *Works* indicate the *Works of Rev. John Wesley, A.M.,* New York, 1831, edited by

John Emory and complete in seven volumes. These *Works* contain quite accurate copies of many of Wesley's writings otherwise practically inaccessible. 3. All references to *Tyerman* refer to the *Life and Times of the Rev. John Wesley, M.A.*, by Rev. Luke Tyerman, New York, 1870, in three volumes. This account is quite detailed and contains many documents not published elsewhere.

This study could not have been completed without the aid of many friends: I wish to express my appreciation to Mr. George D. Brown, librarian of the General Theological Seminary Library, and the Rev. Robert E. Harned, librarian of Drew Theological Seminary. To the Library of Union Theological Seminary, and especially to Miss Cornelia T. Hudson and Miss Laura S. Turnbull, efficient and skilful members of its staff, I am grateful for their never-failing cooperation. Professor John Alfred Faulkner of Drew Theological Seminary has my heartiest thanks for suggesting this theme, reading the proof, and giving many searching criticisms. I am indebted to Professor William A. Dunning of Columbia University, who kindly read my manuscript. Professor F. J. Foakes Jackson, formerly of Cambridge University, England, now of Union Theological Seminary, has placed me under a great debt of gratitude; for he devoted himself unsparingly to my interests in this work. To Professor William Walker Rockwell of Union Theological Seminary am I deeply grateful. During the past four years he has given me without stint of his keen criticism and inspiring counsel.

INTRODUCTION

As a result of the fall of the Puritan ideals in England at the restoration of Charles II, there was a reaction toward immorality. The country, heartily tired of the iron rule of the Saints, was disposed to give itself over to a reign of license. At the time of the Revolution, however, the higher moral ideals began to prevail, and strenuous efforts were made to reform the standard of life and conduct. Christian laymen like the Hon. Robert Boyle, one of the founders of the Royal Society, who formulated the well known "Boyle's Law", worked actively to promote Christian principles. For twenty-eight years Boyle was governor of the Corporation for the Spread of the Gospel in New England, and when he died, he founded and endowed with fifty pounds a year the "Boyle Lectures," for the defense of Christianity against unbelievers.[1] A small company of laymen, led and inspired by Dr. Thomas Bray, an eminent divine of the period, formed themselves into the voluntary "Society for Promoting Christian Knowledge," in order to educate the poor, and send missionaries to America. A little later, in 1701, the "Society for the Propagation of the Gospel" was organized for the more distinct purpose of advancing religion in the plantations.[2]

The reign of Anne was marked by a distinct revival of interest in religion, though unfortunately accompanied by a recrudescence of the High Church spirit opposed to the principles of the Revolution. After the accession of George, I zeal for religion cooled, especially during the long administration of Sir Robert Walpole, whose ruling idea was to leave things as they were and to avoid raising the passion of religious fanaticism. England was occupied with her increasing commercial prosperity, and consequently men desired to maintain the *status quo*.[3] In-

---
[1] *Dictionary of National Biography,* vol. vi, p. 121.
[2] Allen: *History of the Society for Promoting Christian Knowledge.* London, 1898, p. 15.
[3] *Dictionary of National Biography,* vol. lix, p. 203.

deed all religious controversy was avoided as likely to provoke disorder.

Under these circumstances the majority in the Church of England were characterized by indifference and lack of energy.[4] Zeal was repressed rather than encouraged by many of the bishops, "safe" men chosen as supporters of the government. The old High Church party were looked on coldly as Jacobites; and as yet there was no evangelical revival to compensate for their lack of influence.

The Dissenters, recruited from the trading classes, were prospering greatly by the long peace, and were characterized—though with notable exceptions—by a destructive tendency toward deism in religion. The old Puritan zeal had burned itself out; yet the Dissenters showed no desire to return to the Established Church. Dissent was in fact the expression of the feelings of a highly respectable middle class and its ministers under a voluntary system were better paid than the poorer clergy. The government regarded the Church on the whole as useful as a moral police force, encouraging the people to live peacefully under authority. It, however, discouraged manifestations of religious zeal as dangerous to itself and to the nation.

Up to the eighteenth century England had been essentially an agricultural country. Industrialism now began to be a power in the land and with it came the growth of great cities, with the result that the old parochial system collapsed. For the new centers of population no parish was endowed and scarcely a church built. There was no system of public instruction, with the result that a large proportion of the population was in a state of gross ignorance.[5]

In such an England as this were John Wesley and his friends born. When they realized how serious were the conditions, and how supine the Church had become, they became emphatic in expressing their views as to the deplorable condition of the country both in church and state.

---

[4] Wakeman: *History of the Church of England*, chap. 18.
[5] *Vide* Gilbert Slater: *The Making of Modern England*.

CHAPTER I

THE METHODIST VIEW OF EIGHTEENTH CENTURY LIFE

SECTION I. METHODIST DISSATISFACTION WITH THE CUSTOMS AND RELIGION OF THE TIMES

JOHN WESLEY, in a survey of the life round about him, asks: "What is the present characteristic of the English nation?" He answers his own question: "It is ungodliness. This is at present the characteristic of the English nation. Ungodliness is our universal, our constant, our peculiar characteristic." Indeed, the deist of the time was quite a respectable character in Wesley's estimation when compared with the ungodly man of the day.[1] Wesley was very clear in his conviction that no nation had fallen from the first principles of religion quite as low as England. England was contemptuous of all truth, she had an utter disregard for even "Heathen morality," all that should be dear and honorable to rational creatures she neglected.[2]

Wesley did not speak of this lack of piety in general terms. He was specific in his charges. He "once believed the body of English merchants to be men of strictest honesty and honor"; but reluctantly declared he had "lately had more experience."[3] The peasant too was quite ignorant of faith, repentance, holiness; and of religion he could say nothing intelligently.[4] Every class in England—lawyers, gentry, and nobility—came in each for its share of his scathing remarks. He admitted that honest lawyers were to be had; then sarcastically objected: "But are they not thinly spread?"[5] He granted that religion was to be found among the gentry and the nobility, but added: "If you think they are all men of religion, you think very differently

---
[1] *An Estimate of the Manners of the Present Times. Works,* vol. vi, p. 349.
[2] *Works,* vol. v, p. 142.
[3] *Doctrine of Original Sin. Works,* vol. v, p. 516.
[4] *Works,* vol. v, p. 514.
[5] *Ibid.,* vol. v, p. 516.

from your Master, who made no exception of time or nation when he uttered that weighty sentence, 'How difficultly shall they that have riches enter into the kingdom of heaven.' "[6] And very bluntly, in a sermon before the University of Oxford preached at Saint Mary's in the year 1742, he denounced the educated classes in these words: "Brethren, my heart's desire and prayer to God for you is, that ye may be saved from this overflowing ungodliness, and that here its proud waves may be stayed! . . . Ye have not kept yourselves pure. Corrupt are we and also abominable."[7] Thus the learned gownsmen of Oxford were included in this unhappy picture of the times.

The life of the Methodists was a constant protest against that of the age. They disapproved of the gaudy dress then in vogue, and so they adopted drab and somber colors.[8] They advocated self-denial even to the extent of giving up the popular but then expensive luxury of drinking tea.[9] They looked askance at many of the publications of the day, and would have nothing to do with them, as frivolous or obscene.[10] Whether the Methodists were entirely correct in their estimate of the customs and habits of their time we cannot at this point determine. Here we wish simply to show that they were dissatisfied with its moral condition. Like all severe moralists they thought their country was on the downward grade.

SECTION II. METHODIST VIEW OF THE CHURCH AND THE CLERGY

The Methodists spared neither Church nor clergy. Wesley himself was always sparing in his criticism, but other Methodists were not so guarded.[11] Seward, for example, said that the "scarlet whore of Babylon" was not more corrupt in practice or principle than the Church of England.[12] Not that some mem-

---

[6] *Works*, vol. v, p. 517.
[7] *Ibid.*, vol. i, p. 37.
[8] *Ibid.*, vol. vi, p. 545.
[9] *Ibid.*, p. 575.
[10] *Vide Methodist and Mimic*, 1767.
[11] *Works*, vol. vii, p. 273.
[12] Seward: *Journal*, p. 71—quoted in *Wills*, p. 229.

bers of the church were not apprehensive as to its condition.[13] Others drew attention to the severe judgment of popular opinion regarding the Church.[14] Bishop Burnet in 1713 spoke out boldly and said, "I see imminent ruin hanging over the Church, and by consequence, over the whole Reformation. The outward state of things is black enough, God knows; but that which heightens my fears rises chiefly from the inward state into which we are unhappily fallen." The bishop further accused the clergy of being unacquainted with the Bible and maintained that their political interests were a danger to the Church.[15]

The Dissenters were at one as regards the general state of religion. Dr. John Guyse sarcastically remarked that the preachers and the people were content to lay Christ aside. They were in such a state that they needed a mediator no longer.[16] Abraham Taylor, an independent minister at Little Moorfields, London, stated that the people had no idea of what the Holy Spirit was. All who professed to rely upon the aid of the Spirit were ridiculed.[17] Isaac Watts claimed that the decline of vital religion within the hearts of men was a matter for mournful observation among all that laid the cause of God to heart.[18] His advice for a remedy of conditions was to urge ministers to make it their business to insist upon those subjects which were inward and spiritual, and which went by the name of "experimental religion."[19] Churchmen, Dissenters, and Methodists thus united together in their criticism of the Church, as representing the religion of the majority of the nation.

Wesley and others felt that the weakness of the Church lay in the moral and intellectual weakness of the clergy, whom he describes as "dull, heavy, blockish ministers; men of no life, no spirit, no readiness of thought; who are consequently the jest of every pert fool, every lively, airy coxcomb they meet."[20]

---

[13] *Serious Address to the Members of the Church of England, passim.*
[14] *Ibid.*, p. 5.
[15] Jackson: *Centenary of Wesleyan Methodism*, pp. 14-15.
[16] *Ibid., op. cit.*, p. 19ff.
[17] *Ibid.*, p. 23.
[18] Watts: *An Humble Attempt Toward the Revival* . . . pref., pp. 2-3.
[19] *Ibid.*, p. 55.
[20] *Works*, vol. vi, pp. 2-3.

Bishop Gibson replied to Whitefield's strictures in his Pastoral letter.[21] They had little grip on their people. Their parishioners were held as by a "rope of sand."[22] Taylor in his *Defence of Methodism* asserted that the clergy, as a rule, were worldly and ignorant political organizers rather than pastors. He maintained that the Church had been oppressive ever since the days of Elizabeth. To prove this he inserted a list of good men sacrificed to its system.[23] But the greatest scandal in the eyes of the Methodists was the drunkenness prevalent in the clerical profession. Thus at Newtownbarry, in Ireland, the members of the Methodist Society would not go to the parish Church on account of the drinking habits of the clergyman.[24] At Yarmouth Wesley describes the people as "being full of prejudice against the clergy for this reason."[25] Joseph Crownley, a layman, dared not hear a drunkard preach or read prayers.[26] He and others appealed to the Wesleys as leaders of their cause, asking whether they were obliged to submit themselves to the ministrations of an intemperate clergyman. At Wednesbury, a gentleman rode up to a group to which John Wesley was speaking, and after insulting him sought to trample upon the people with his horse. Wesley found that he was a drunken clergyman.[27]

Nor was intemperance the only fault. Charles Wesley was shocked at their behavior during divine service at Christ Church.[28] John Wesley spoke of some clergy as being "in the high road to hell." Many, in his estimation, were wolves in sheep's clothing. They were characterized as: common swearers, open drunkards, notorious Sabbath breakers—"and such are many parochial ministers of this day." Wesley could not and would not urge his followers to worship under such men as these. Every man must judge for himself.[29] So in answer

---
[21] Gibson: *Pastoral Letter*, p. 24.
[22] Outram: p. 125.
[23] T. Taylor: *Defence of Meth. passim.*
[24] *Jour.*, vol. v, p. 328.
[25] *Ibid.*, p. 245.
[26] Jackson: *Life of Charles Wesley*, p. 508.
[27] *Jour.*, vol. i, p. 75.
[28] C. Wesley: *Jour.*, vol. i, p. 380.
[29] *Works*, vol. ii, p. 325.

to the questions of his followers as to whether they should sit under the ministrations of a drunken or immoral clergyman, Wesley replied, "it is the duty of every private Christian to obey his spiritual pastor, by either doing or leaving undone anything of an indifferent nature; anything that is in no way determined in the word of God."[30] This was an indirect way of saying, that in the important things, it was not necessary for a Methodist to obey a bad clergyman.

Wesley was always ready to acknowledge the merits of worthy clergymen. As, for instance, when Mr. Vowler at Saint Agnes preached "two such thundering sermons" as he had scarce heard in twenty years. Wesley's comment is that God was very good to the sinners of Saint Agnes.[31] Indeed, whenever he was accused of being abusive he took pains to emphatically deny the charge.[32]

Such was the general opinion of the clergy. If it was true, it was only true in part. For example, in *Methodism Displayed*, Bate says that the statements adverse to the character of churchmen were not worth noticing, because they were such good people.[33] Again, Bishop Porteus in his *Life of Archbishop Secker* says: "The dignity of his form . . . inspired at all times respect and awe, but peculiarly when he engaged in any of the more solemn functions of religion; into which he entered with such earnestness and warmth, with so just a consciousness of the place he was in, and the business he was about as seemed to raise him above himself, and added new life and spirit to the natural gracefulness of his appearance."[34] Then as always there were good and bad clergy; the question was which element preponderated?

The Methodists, perhaps not unnaturally, took a decidedly gloomy view of the ordinary life of their age and especially of the condition of the Church. Rightly or wrongly the verse they placed upon the tombstone of J. W. Fletcher, of Madeley, repre-

---

[30] *Works*, vol. ii, p. 327.
[31] *Jour.*, vol. iv, p. 234.
[32] J. Wesley: *Letter to Author of Enthusiasm*, p. 10.
[33] Bate: *Meth. Displayed*, p. 37.
[34] *Life of Secker*, p. liv.

sented their sentiments: "All day long, have I stretched out my hands to a disobedient and gainsaying people."[35] They might be wrong, but this was their conviction. Individuals with such convictions act. The Methodists were no exception. Life in their view must be completely changed, the Church purified, religion must again come to its own. One outcome of this conviction and action was to arouse in some a desire to go out from the Church as established.

---

[35] *Life of J. Fletcher, Works,* vol. vi, p. 483.

CHAPTER II

THE CHURCHMAN'S VIEW OF EIGHTEENTH CENTURY LIFE

The Methodists took no flattering view of the Church, and many churchmen were equally ready with their criticisms. The reason for this antipathy is to be found in the prevalent dread of what was then known as "enthusiasm."

Section I. Enthusiasm

"Enthusiasm," as used in the eighteenth century, meant not zeal for a cause, but possession by a spirit resembling insanity. When the Methodists first began to preach, certain extraordinary manifestations accompanied their efforts. Thus Wesley recorded that while he was preaching a woman in his audience was affected; "her teeth gnashed together, her knees smote each other, her body trembled exceedingly."[1] At another time he told of how he was preaching and "one sunk down, and another, and another; some cried aloud in an agony of prayer." One young man and one young woman were brought into a house nearby where they continued in violent physical agony.[2] At another time twenty-six were affected, and they all seemed worse than as if they had been afflicted with hysteria or epileptic fits.[3] At Kingswood, during the communion service, one woman dropped down as dead while she was taking the sacrament.[4] When preaching took place at Newgate prison, the entire prison "rang with cries."[5] A Mrs. Means was disputing with Wesley. On the way home she felt the "piercing of a sword," and before she could get to her home, she could not avoid crying out aloud, even in the street.[6]

---

[1] *Jour.*, vol. ii, p. 152.
[2] Overton: *Life of Wesley*, p. 112.
[3] *Jour.*, vol. ii, p. 222.
[4] *Ibid.*, vol. ii, p. 232.
[5] *Ibid.*, p. 185.
[6] *Ibid.*, p. 148.

These occurred not only among the immediate followers of Wesley, but even among those who were actually hostile to the movement. John Wilde, who said that none but hypocrites had these spells, had one himself. Another woman at Long Lane always became angry at those who pretended to be in fits. She also had a spell of great agony.[7] At Baldwin Street Church, a Quaker came to see the fraud and to expose it. "He dropped down thunderstruck," and "his agony was terrible to behold."[8] A prominent churchman, who also wished to see the fraud, came thither and in turn was overcome.[9]

Not only under the preaching of John Wesley did these events happen. Other men, including Whitefield and sometimes Charles Wesley, found their hearers thus affected. Even Ralph Erskine, a minister of Scotland, who was in no way connected with the Wesleys, had wonderful effects attend his preaching.[10]

This peculiar type of religious excitement was not limited to the early days of the Methodist movement. In 1785, John Mance, an old man, sank down at a service at Saint Ives. He was carried out of the church and died immediately.[11] It would seem that "enthusiasm" in this case had caused heart failure. In 1786, a service was described in which all pray aloud at the same time, some scream, some use indecent expressions in prayer, some drop down dead and then stand up again and shout "glory!"[12]

The attitude of Wesley toward all of these doings appears to have varied. He preached occasionally the terrors of the Lord in the strongest manner he was able.[13] Beau Nash, the famous Master of the Ceremonies at Bath, told Wesley to his face that his preaching frightened people out of their wits.[14] George Whitefield, who doubted the reality of this enthusiasm, was convinced when he came to Wesley. Thereupon Wesley

---

[7] *Jour.*, pp. 376-377.
[8] *Ibid.*, p. 187.
[9] *Ibid.*, p. 190ff.
[10] Moore: *Life of Wesley*, vol. i, p. 364.
[11] *Jour.*, vol. iii, p. 109.
[12] *Ibid.*, vol. vii, p. 153.
[13] *Ibid.*, vol. iii, p. 344.
[14] *Ibid.*, vol. ii, p. 212.

FROM THE CHURCH OF ENGLAND

remarked: "From this time I trust we shall all suffer God to carry on his own work in the way that pleaseth him."[15] It would thus seem that Wesley encouraged this enthusiasm.

Yet in the realm of dreams and visions he was more cautious. At the Fishponds, Wesley cautioned his hearers against dreams, revelations, visions, tears, or any involuntary effects upon their bodies. Yet even while he was doing this people dropped down.[16] Wesley admitted that he had seen dreams change people; but he would not judge them to be Christians on the basis of dreams, but on the whole subsequent tenor of their lives.[17] Agitations, visions, or dreams were not certain evidence of true conversion to God. They might accompany such conversion, but they were not the sole evidence of its reality.[18] Yet the conference of 1745, under the influence of Wesley, went on record saying that it did not intend to discourage these visions and dreams, and declaring "we cannot deny that saving faith is often given in dreams or visions of the night."[19] Thus although dreams and visions were admitted, they were not considered necessary for vital religion.

On the other hand, Wesley was outspoken against the more extravagant forms of enthusiasm. Some said they felt the blood of Christ running upon their arms, or going down their throats, or poured like warm water upon their breasts or hearts. Wesley briefly dismissed all this as the result of a heated imagination.[20] Mary Watson took part in a Methodist meeting by reciting the following verse:

> "Why do these cares my soul divide,
> If thou indeed hast set me free?
> Why am I thus, if God hath died,
> If God hath died to purchase me?
> Around me clouds of darkness roll;
> In deepest night I still walk on:
> Heavily moves my damnèd soul,
> My comfort and my God are gone."

This religious melancholia Wesley would not tolerate. Mary

---
[15] *Ibid.*, vol. ii, p. 240.
[16] *Ibid.*, vol. ii, p. 226.
[17] *Ibid.*, vol. ii, p. 203.
[18] Moore: *op cit.*, vol. i, p. 363.
[19] *Min. of 1745. Works*, vol. v, p. 200.
[20] *Jour.*, vol. iii, p. 44.

Watson was rebuked and made to keep quiet.[21] At Bristol five persons raged in a room where Wesley was trying to preach. He would not have his voice interrupted, or the attention of his congregation diverted; so he ordered these persons to be removed while he preached. Wesley would not permit enthusiasm to interfere with his services.[22] Later on he took the steps to give his preachers formal directions to assist them in overcoming enthusiasm.

The problem that faced Wesley was the one ever recurring problem that had come before the Church fathers whenever a belief in a new and final outpouring of the Spirit arose. As early as the second century the same phenomenon occurred among some zealots who hailed the appearance of the Paraclete in Phrygia, and surrendered themselves to his guidance. These were known as Montanists, and their enthusiasm and prophesyings were attributed to the devil by the bishops, who after vainly attempting to exorcise the spirit by which they were possessed put them out of the Church.[23]

In Luther's day a claim to direct inspiration, which was quite similar to that made by the Montanists, was made by the so-called *Zwickau Prophets,* and was stoutly opposed by Luther, who endeavored to silence them by his ridicule.[24] The Quaker movement, resting on a similar claim to miracles, prophecies, and the direct inspiration of its adherents, was opposed by the organized churches both in England and America on the ground of blasphemy.[25] As a member of the Church, Wesley was disposed to assume the same attitude toward these claims of direct inspiration and this enthusiasm.

Wesley not only acted, but he also wrote and preached against enthusiasm. In a letter to Miss Ritchie, he makes his personal position quite clear. "I am rarely led by impressions, but generally by reason and the Scripture. I see abundantly more than I feel."[26] When it came to a definition of enthusiasm,

---
[21] *Jour.*, vol. ii, p. 303.
[22] *Ibid.*, vol. ii, p. 324.
[23] Eusebius: *Church History,* Book v, chap. xviff.
[24] *New Schaff-Herzog Ency.,* 1908, vol. i, p. 162.
[25] F. S. Turner: *The Quakers.* London, 1889, pp. 120 and 168.
[26] *Works,* vol. vii, p. 183.

Wesley appeared to be upon nearly a common ground with the clergy. "I was with two persons who I doubt are properly enthusiasts. For first, they think to attain the end without the means; which is enthusiasm so called. Again, they think themselves inspired of God and are not. But false imaginary inspiration is enthusiasm."[27] In preaching, he declared that there was a real spirit of God, and an imaginary one, which enthusiasts failed to distinguish and therefore were deceived.[28] In addition to this, he said that some expected to attain their ends by the supernatural intervention of God's power. This was not the case: "If we have the means, if we can do the given task ourself, it is our duty to do so. God will not miraculously do for us what we should do for ourselves."[29] He declared that thinking men meant by enthusiasm a sort of religious madness; a false imagination of being inspired of God; a fancying of one's self to be under the influence of the Holy Ghost when in fact one is not.[30]

Many Methodists shared in the distrust of "enthusiasm"; as one of them writes, he had seen enthusiasm and error creep into his church, obliging him to rebuke the leaders because they were not more vigorous in combating it.[31] They should have, he remarks, restrained and not fostered the unprofitable emotions of "screaming, hallowing, and jumping, and the stepping and singing of merry senseless airs. These have often prejudiced true and vital religion."[32] A *Life of Wesley* denies that Methodism was responsible for these excesses, though the author blamed Wesley for not being on his guard better against them.[33]

To enable the reader to decide what was the cause of this "enthusiasm," we cannot do better than draw instances of it as evidence. These cases, which would now be ascribed to insanity, were by Wesley assigned to the direct operation of God or of Satan.

---

[27] *Jour.*, vol. ii, p. 130.
[28] *Works*, vol. i, p. 333.
[29] *Ibid.*, vol. i, p. 335.
[30] *Ibid.*, vol. v, p. 76.
[31] *Works*, vol. i, p. 334.
[32] Wesleyan Methodist: *Meth. Error.* pref.
[33] Hampson: *Life of Wesley*, vol. ii, p. 137.

In October, 1739, he was called in to see a woman taken ill the evening before. She was in a fury, gnashed her teeth and raved, but after two days was calm.[34] A certain Alice Miller, a girl fifteen years old, fell into a trance, but here there was no raving.[35]

In such instances the only remedy was prayer. Again, Sally Jones, of Kingswood, who was very ignorant, was under a spell. "The thousand distortions of her whole body showed how the dogs of hell were gnawing at her heart." She declared she belonged to the devil, and prayed to him to come and take her. Wesley began to sing a hymn, then prayed, and this quieted her.[36] A Mrs. Crompton, though enraged at Wesley's preaching, fell also in one of these spells, but Wesley prayed with her and she declared her sins forgiven.[37] Dr. James Munroe, chief physician of Bethlehem Hospital, once sent a case of madness to Wesley, and Wesley said the patient would recover if she only would trust God.[38] Yet in no case would he admit that such manifestations were the results of disordered minds. He maintained that these persons were in perfect health, and that the spell had come upon them suddenly. It was Satan tearing them. Nor would he have agreed with Southey's explanation that Wesley, "like Mesmer and his disciples, had produced a new disease, and he accounted for it by a theological theory instead of a physical one."[39]

One is not, however, surprised to hear Wesley ask in the Conference of 1778: "Why do so many of our preachers fall into nervous disorders?" and simply suggesting that it was the strain of zeal and emotion reached in the meetings, which was more than Methodist preachers could endure.

Modern biographers of Wesley, like Overton, consider that exhibitions of this enthusiasm can be accounted for by distraught emotion in excited crowds; and that Wesley was often imposed

---

[34] *Jour.*, vol. iv, p. 300.
[35] *Ibid.*, vol. iv, p. 347.
[36] *Ibid.*, vol. ii, p. 288.
[37] *Ibid.*, vol. ii, p. 147.
[38] *Ibid.*, vol. ii, p. 280.
[39] Southey: *Life of Wesley*, vol. i, p. 214.

upon by them.[40] Cadman's theory is that John Wesley so controlled his own powerful emotion, that the people who listened could not stand the strain and were obliged to give vent to their feelings and fell down overcome by them.[41]

Modern psychology explains these actions, in part, by attributing them to fresh sensory elements that often play a part in conversion. Dr. Coe reminds us that the tone of the preacher's voice; the rhythm, volume, and melody of the revival songs; organic sensations, such as thrills, tingles, shudders; very possibly now and then sexual sensations not recognized as such—all of these must be reckoned with in connection with conversion.[42] He says: "It is clear, for example, that a bold, commanding tone and manner on the part of some preachers produce an effect over and above what they say."[43] Wesley, by his commanding tone and manner and the ideas he suggested, aroused the excitability of his uneducated hearers and caused manifestations of enthusiasm which would not have occupied people of better disciplined minds.

But for many Methodists these experiences were essential. Their conversion would not have been complete without some exceptional manifestation. And the average convert would testify thus: "In this violent agony I continued four hours . . . I, who had nothing but devils to drag me down to hell, now found I had angels to guide me to my reconciled father."[44] Rightly or wrongly, the average Methodist valued such an experience as a necessary assurance of salvation.

Having seen what enthusiasm was, we must inquire how it appeared in the eyes of the outside world.

SECTION II. THE CHURCH VIEW OF ENTHUSIASM

Religious controversy had been going on in England ever since the days of Henry VIII; and at the opening of the eight-

---

[40] Overton: *Life of Wesley*, p. 113.
[41] Cadman: *Three Religious Leaders of Oxford*, section on Wesley.
[42] *Psychology of Religion*, p. 157.
[43] *Ibid.*, p. 158.
[44] *Jour.*, vol. i, p. 110.

eenth century it was hoped that it had been allayed by the revolution settlement. People dreaded its renewal, and were prejudiced against any who seemed likely to revive it by their preaching. Josiah Tucker expressed the popular view, "The last century furnishes us with a melancholy proof in our own country. Whosoever will be at the trouble of comparing the first rise of those troubles which at last overturned the constitution and ruined the nation, will see too great a similitude between them and the present risings of enthusiastic rant not to apprehend the danger that, unless proper precautions be taken in time, the remote consequences may be fatal." The whole nation was open to new ideas; enthusiasm was advancing rapidly.[45] In other words, the new enthusiasm seemed likely to cause trouble as it had done in the past. Churchmen, disgusted by the excesses of Quakers, Moravians, and French Prophets, included the Methodists among other disturbers of the political peace.[46] They were further provoked by Dissenting publications defending schism. Neal's four volumes entitled, *The History of the Puritans,* and Calamy's works nettled the Churchmen.[47]

In addition to the trials of controversy, the Church, in its controversy with rationalism, had in a measure fallen under its influence. This being the case, one need not be surprised to hear that "religion is a wise, a still, a silent thing, that consists not in freaks of fancy, and whirlwinds of passions; but in a divine temper of mind, and a universal resignation of our wills to God; and this not only in intermittent fits of passion, but in the midst of cool thoughts and calm deliberations."[48] Could anything be farther from the Methodist "enthusiasm" than this cool rationalistic frame of mind?

Thus many Churchmen were conscientiously opposed to "enthusiasm" and those who practiced it, as contrary to the spirit of what they conceived to be religion, and as subversive of the discipline of the Church.[49] Methodism was called a

---

[45] Tucker: *Conduct of Whitefield,* p. 11.
[46] Evans: *History of Enthusiasm, passim.*
[47] *Ibid.,* pref., p. xvii.
[48] Scott: *Fine Picture of Methodism,* p. 14.
[49] Free: *Sermon, 1758,* p. 7.

species of enthusiasm which drew attention so strongly to some particular doctrines and duties of revealed religion, and fixed it upon these doctrines so intently as to exclude the other parts of religion, and even morality itself.[50]

The opponents of Methodism demanded, not unreasonably, evidence in support of their claims. Samuel Wesley, the older brother of John Wesley, voiced this demand when he said to his brother: "Your followers fall into agonies. I confess it. They are freed from it after you have prayed over them. Granted. They say it is the Lord's doing. I own they say so. Dear brother, where is your ocular demonstration? Where, indeed, the rational proof?"[51] Samuel Wesley here felt the lack of evidence. The Churchmen felt that God did not manifest himself by extraordinary acts of his power; but in his regular Providence should men be the more apt to find him?[52] To deny this was likely to lead to a rejection of the plain and practical precepts of Christianity; to follow after vain delusions which encouraged fanatical conceit.[53]

John Green stated the point clearly when he objected to the Methodist claims: "You have received some extraordinary manifestation of God's favor and discoveries of his will, and you require us to believe them; give us then some reasonable and satisfactory proof, on which our belief may be properly grounded; otherwise you are much too arbitrary and assuming in what you require. . . . put us not off with flights, raptures, and assertions."[54] This seems to be a just demand by a serious, reasoning Churchman.

The Methodists gave great offense by their pretension to intimate acquaintance with God and heavenly things.[55] To many no illusion could be more diabolical than that a man should hearken to the suggestions which he miscalled conscience and the spirit of God within him, in preference to the plain revelation of God's will in the Scripture. The law of nature; right rea-

---

[50] *Essay on Character of Methodism*, p. 11.
[51] Letter quoted in Moore's *Life of Wesley*, vol. i, p. 372.
[52] *Principles and Practices of Methodism*, p. 13.
[53] H. Smith: *Methodist Conceit*, p. 22ff.
[54] *Principles and Practices of Methodism*, p. 20.
[55] Kirby: p. 3.

son; these should be the guides for man's action.[56] Many Churchmen had the idea that Methodist enthusiasm consisted in uncommon degrees of illumination which showed itself in "a religious distemper" and often in a "downright frenzy." "It pretends to hold an intimate communion with God. . . . it sets up for voices and visions and dreams, for new lights and new paths, in derogation and opposition to the written word. . . . It aims at pitches of devotion, at heights and ecstasies, besides the common rate. . . . it despises the rational way of serving God by sober signs and solid effects of unaffected piety and the conscientious practise of good Christian morality."[57]

The argument ran: If the Methodists have direct revelation, why do they not give proof? If the Methodists have this direct revelation, why do they live bad lives? The anonymous author of *Principles and Practices of Methodists* said that the Methodists for all their outward signs of enthusiasm, "yet seem not, so far as people can judge from outward demeanor, to be reclaimed from habits of vice . . . though they have experienced such agonies of mind and body . . . yet several of them still continue to give offense to serious persons, by a loose, disorderly behavior."[58]

The zeal of Methodists certainly led them into indiscretions which provoked the accusations that they had "inherited the extraordinary light of the Gnostics," as Downes ironically put it; but in all of their accusations against the enthusiasm of the Methodists their opponents never seemed to have been able to substantiate the charge of immorality.[59]

The enthusiasm of George Whitefield drew forth vigorous protests from the clergy, especially when he claimed the sanction of the Holy Ghost for his preaching. He was challenged to produce evidence for this claim.[60] Whitefield and his associates caused further offense by their depreciation of reason.[61]

Whitefield's journals were the cause of much offense.

---

[56] Evans: *History of Enthusiasm*, pref. p. xiv.
[57] Grey: *Address to Lay-Meth.*, p. 13ff.
[58] P. 31.
[59] *Methodism Examined*, p. 12.
[60] *Observations on Mr. Seagrave's Conduct*, p. 36.
[61] John Green: *Principles and Practices*, p. 11.

Thoughtful clergymen hated them. "Don't you think they are all damned cant?" Wesley was asked. His inquirer felt that these journals dealt with "joy and stuff, and inward feeling."[62] The contents of these journals were quite repulsive in the eyes of sober-minded clergymen. As for instance when Whitefield rather extravagantly said that it was good providence that he and his sister-in-law could not agree when they worked together at Bell Inn, his enemies could not contain themselves. "He has certainly struck a bold note," they said, "in making God the direct author of the ridiculous squabbles between him and his sister."[63]

Josiah Tucker in his work entitled, *The Genuine Secret Memoires of George Whitefield,* reached the high water mark of bitterness in his ungenerous allusions to Whitefield having been a "common drawer" in a public house in early life. "There," said Tucker, "he appeared to be acting in his proper sphere, and there are several notable improvements in the profession ascribed to him; he is said to have frothed a mug of ale a tenth deeper than any tapster in the three kingdoms, to have been the first to have soaped the edges of the pot, in order to make the beer retain its head."[64] Whitefield's narrative of his own birth and the premonitions to his mother telling her of what great comfort he should be to her was ridiculed by Tucker.[65] He does not scruple to impute much to Whitefield that does not appear in his journal, but can be inferred only by reading between the lines.[66] Tucker ends by saying that Whitefield's journals did not show that he had any intimate communion with God; but rather with the devil, and if he was inspired at all, he was inspired only by the devil.[67]

It must be confessed that Whitefield's journals do give an opening for attack; and when it was declared that when Whitefield left the movement one more enthusiast was disposed of, one cannot forbear thinking that this was correct.[68] Neverthe-

---

[62] *Jour.*, vol. ii, p. 319.
[63] *Methodism Dissected*, p. 19.
[64] *Op. cit.*, p. 33.
[65] *Ibid.*, p. 17.
[66] Pp. 39-40 and 54-55.
[67] P. 11.
[68] Evans: *History of Enthusiasm*, p. 111.

less, when the attackers of these journals went so far as to accuse Whitefield of immorality and his writings as tainted with obscenity, they brought no evidence to prove their contention.

The opposition of the Church to enthusiasm was not based upon a doctrinal basis alone. It objected to certain enthusiastic habits which the Methodists indulged in. It did not like the disposition to allegorize and spiritualize the most plain and obvious texts which was common among the Methodists,[69] and the practice of claiming that extemporaneous prayer was inherently of a higher order than set forms as proceeding from the direct influence of the Holy Ghost.[70]

Few wished to have their children come under the influence of Methodist enthusiasm. It displeased parents to hear such language from them after their having been to hear John Wesley: "God has pardoned my sins through the blood of the atonement." They complained not without a cause: "that the minds of youth should be imbued with this tincture of fanaticism before they know how to distinguish truth from falsehood, when reason is beginning to dawn and the passions to play, is an evil, pregnant with most fatal consequences."[71]

A clergyman accused the Methodists of preaching that the millennium was soon to come, in which the Methodists, as the saints, were going to live in peace upon the earth.[72] In this he misunderstood Methodism as did those who classed the Methodists with Cotton Mather of Boston,[73] or confounded their enthusiasm with the fanaticism of a certain Christian George, who after claiming to be a prophet in North Carolina, shot up the town where he lived, killed the justice of the peace, indulged in adultery, etc.[74]

Rumor gained in intensity as it traveled. When the reports of the Methodists reached the bishops they were doubtless exaggerated. The bishops, as might be expected, opposed the current enthusiasm. On the frontispiece of Bishop Gibson's

---

[69] Nightingale: p. 258.
[70] Evans: *History of Enthusiasm*, pref. p. xv.
[71] Wills: pp. 130ff.
[72] *Letter from a Clergyman to One of His Parishioners*, p. 72ff.
[73] Evans: *Op. cit.*, pref., p. xix.
[74] Grey: *Serious Address to Lay Methodists*, appendix, p. 22.

work, *Observations of Methodism,* is a picture of a Methodist service, in which are faints, love making, witches, devils, rabbits, and the like. This shows the episcopal conception of Methodism in some degree, but it is nevertheless quite untrue to fact.

In this same work the bishop attacks the Methodists in a more orderly fashion. He objects to the flowery language used in their writings, to their communications with God, to their extravagant flights and illusions.[75] Bishop Lavington was not as moderate as Gibson. Of this enthusiasm he said: "If there be anything in it exceeding the power of nature, known or secret; anything beyond the force of distemper, or of imagination and enthusiasm artfully worked up. . . . I see no reason against concluding that it is the work of some evil spirit; a sort of magical operation, or other diabolical illusion."[76] The Methodists never forgave Lavington for this senseless onslaught almost wholly unsupported by evidence. Vincent Perronet roundly rebuked the bishop and declared it to be scandalous that he should claim the emotions of the Methodists to be physical instead of spiritual.[77]

In spite of this able defense, the clergy held to their opinion. They hated the intrusion of the Methodist preacher into sick rooms where the patient was excited with new terrors or with groundless hopes.[78] They continued to think of conversion as the sum of a number of bodily passions; as an abnormality taking place in experience.[79] They still insisted that enthusiasm was a danger to the throne as puritanism had been in the days of Oliver Cromwell; and as such they maintained that it ought to be suppressed as seditious.[80] Certainly Whitefield's preaching tended to make men Dissenters rather than Churchmen.[81]

Thus most of the clergy had little sympathy with enthusiasm, and many opposed it openly. It was, in fact, a leading

---

[75] P. 17ff.
[76] *Enthusiasm of Methodists and Papists Compared,* p. 398.
[77] *Third Letter to Author of Enthus. of Meth. and Papists Compared, passim.*
[78] Wills: p. 100.
[79] Scott: *Op. cit.,* p. 6.
[80] Roe: P. 289.
[81] Overton: *Evangelical Revival in 18th Century,* p. 154.

30 THE SEPARATION OF THE METHODISTS

cause in the severance of Methodism from the Church. In a contest between two entirely incompatible ideals, one must yield or depart from the other. Neither the Churchmen nor the Methodists would yield.

Section III. Methodist Attempts to Check Extreme Enthusiasm

One cannot but surmise that John Wesley saw the situation, and in spite of his inconsistent stand on the matter of enthusiasm in the abstract, was determined that fanaticism in the concrete should not dominate his societies.

The first ultra-enthusiasts to trouble the early Methodists were the French Prophets. These sought refuge in England after the revocation of the Edict of Nantes.[82] But little is known of them until the year 1706. In that year three French Camisards came to England. J. Cavalier, who was portrayed as a villain, trickster, and scamp, was the first. Durant Fage, "a mechanic who gave off incoherent stuff for prophecy," was the second. Elias Marion, who was a good actor, was the third. All three were said to be Roman Catholics. They joined the French church at Savoy. They played fraud upon many, and when they were discovered suddenly received orders from the Holy Spirit to return to France. Nevertheless, they had a good time before they went, for they were lionized and rode about in coaches.[83] Gilbert Burnet said that for the most part these "prophets" were poor, ignorant people.[84] This was the first appearance of the French Prophets; but at the beginning of the Methodist movement they came into greater prominence.

The French Prophets not only tried to ingratiate themselves into the good graces of the Methodists, but they troubled the Nonconformists as well. Leger narrates the following in this connection: "Le mercredi précédent à la clôture d'une réunion annuelle de Nonconformists, d'éminénts prédicateurs haranguaient l'auditoire quand se dresse dans la tribune une femme qui, dépouillant ses vêtements de dessus, apparaît dans une sorte

---

[82] Leger: *Jeunesse de Wesley*, p. 421.
[83] Evans: *Op. cit.*, pp. 97-100.
[84] Quoted in Southey's *Life of Wesley*, vol. i, p. 458.

d'effrayant cilice; elle répand des cendres sur sa tête; elle gesticule comme une forcenée. On lève la séance; on expulse les imposteurs; la foule les crible de boue, et s'amasse si nombreuse que le Sheriff et la force publique sont obligés dans la soirée, de la disperse."[85] The Nonconformists were not in sympathy with the French Prophets. So next these "prophets" turned to the Moravians. They sent deputies to Zinzendorf. But the Moravians would have nothing to do with them because they neglected the sacrament. So in 1739 they sought to convert the Methodists to their way of thinking. The enthusiasm displayed by the Methodists had, perhaps, made them think that the Methodists were prepared for their way of doing things.[86]

The "prophets" were typical enthusiasts. To come under the operation of the Holy Spirit they put themselves into postures and agitations. They shook their heads and whirled in a violent manner until a vertigo seized them. They threw their hands and tossed to and fro beyond the wild pranks of any wild man, "sometimes whistling, and then singing and laughing, piping, drumming, screaming, etc." Such were their actions.

Their doctrine was equally radical. The millennium was soon to come—in fact, within a few months. Christ was to appear personally.[87] The French church denounced these men, but their influence continued to spread. Sir Richard Bulkley and John Lacy, Esq., were won over to their cause. These men set themselves to the work of prophesying, and said that Dr. Ems, a friend of theirs, should rise from the grave May 25, 1708. Many came out to see this resurrection. When the event did not come off, the people were inclined to doubt, and to overcome this doubt Sir Richard and his friend John Lacy threatened with massacre all who should oppose them.[88]

Although these "prophets" were repudiated by some, nevertheless, some believed on them. Mr. Hollis, of Wickham, favored these people and maintained their superiority to the prophets of the Old Testament. He tried to influence Charles

---
[85] *Jeunesse de Wesley*, p. 424.
[86] Southey: vol. i, pp. 241-242.
[87] Evans: p. 100.
[88] *Ibid.*, pp. 105-107.

Wesley in the matter, but Charles Wesley was too good a Churchman to be thus easily influenced. One night Charles Wesley slept with Hollis. While they were undressing "he fell into violent agitations and gabbled like a turkey cock." Charles was frightened, but was not convinced; for he began to exorcise Hollis, saying, "thou deaf and dumb devil, come out of him." Hollis evidently did not like Charles Wesley's uncomplimentary attitude toward his religious experience, so he soon recovered from his fit of inspiration.[89] A little later on, Charles Wesley had a discussion with one of the societies concerning these French Prophets. At the conclusion of the discussion Charles Wesley asked, "Who is on God's side? Who for the old prophets rather than the new? Let them follow me. They followed me into the preaching room."[90] Thus Charles Wesley and his followers definitely broke with the French Prophets.

The attempts to influence John Wesley were as great a failure as with his brother Charles. He went to hear a prophetess who leaned back in her chair and gabbled very much. She gave deep sighs. Wesley was far from being impressed with her.[91] Then he came out in public and denounced these "prophets" as "properly enthusiasts." He said they thought themselves to be inspired by God, but were not. False, imaginary inspiration is enthusiasm.[92] This type of inspiration the French Prophets had. And when Wesley was accused of favoring the French Prophets, the question was bluntly put to him: "Do you not commend the French Prophets?" To this question he categorically answered, "No."[93]

In this way the leaders of Methodism broke absolutely with these French Prophets and the movement was saved from a fanaticism of the extremest type. Fanaticism might easily have spoiled the movement for any practical usefulness right at its beginning.

The second ultra enthusiasts to trouble Methodism were

---

[89] Moore: *Life of Wesley*, vol. i, p. 347.
[90] *Ibid.*, pp. 385-386.
[91] Southey: vol. i, p. 242.
[92] *Ibid.*, p. 241.
[93] *Works*, vol. vii, p. 402.

FROM THE CHURCH OF ENGLAND 33

of a different sort. They were Methodists; namely, Thomas Maxfield and George Bell. Both had been permitted to preach by Wesley. Maxfield was put in charge of the Methodist society at the Foundry for a season. Not long after Wesley left the Foundry, and some of the people claimed dreams, visions, and impressions, as they thought, from God. Maxfield did not discourage, but rather encouraged them. He believed that they were signs of the highest grace. Wesley at once took a position emphatically opposed to this type of enthusiasm.[94] He told Maxfield plainly that these inner emotions, mysticism, would not be tolerated. He condemned screaming, unintelligible words, etc. The upshot of the whole matter was that Maxfield left the movement.[95]

Wesley had difficulty in the matter. The kind of people who composed this earlier Methodist movement was such as would be prone to follow enthusiasm of Maxfield's type. It had seized a hold upon Methodism. One hundred and six members left the society at the Foundry when Maxfield went out.[96] At that same time there was a decrease in the total membership of the Methodist societies from about 2,800 to 2,200. Wesley attributed this in part to the work of Maxfield.[97]

George Bell was a friend of Maxfield. Of the two he was the more fanatical. His admirers professed the gift of healing. They attempted to cure blindness and to raise the dead.[98] Bell prophesied the end of the world. Near Saint Luke's Hospital, on February 28, 1763, he was arrested and committed to prison. Wesley saw to it that he left Methodism. Southey called him an "ignorant enthusiast" who became an "ignorant infidel." He died at a ripe old age, posing as a reformer.[99]

Wesley in this way broke with these two fanatics regardless of what it might cost him. He thought them full of self-conceit, stubborn, and impatient of contradiction.[100] It was an act of

---

[94] *Jour.*, vol. v, p. 11.
[95] *Ibid.*, vol. iv, p. 535ff.
[96] *Ibid.*, vol. v, p. 40.
[97] *Ibid.*, vol. v, p. 155.
[98] *Methodist Magazine*, 1790, p. 42.
[99] *Jour.*, vol. v, p. 9, note iii.
[100] *Ibid.*, vol. v, p. 54.

34 THE SEPARATION OF THE METHODISTS

wisdom and statesmanship for Wesley to see clearly enough to rid his movement of such men as these. We cannot agree with Hampson, when he stated that Wesley gave too much encouragement to these enthusiasts.[101] He did not. He put them out, and thus saved Methodism from becoming weak with fanaticism and ultra radicalism.

Section IV. Methodism and Mysticism

Methodism met enthusiasm in yet one other form—mysticism. This had to be met and dealt with. In 1739, upon returning to Fetter Lane, Wesley found that Philip Henry Molther, private tutor to the son of Count Zinzendorf, had been talking to his people and confusing them; so that they were ready to deny all religion.[102] The teaching that was making for all of this confusion was the Moravian doctrine of "stillness." Wesley said that the Moravians owned they never had a living faith. They were going to be "still" until they gained it. They taught that one should leave off the means of grace; stay away from church; cease to communicate; stop reading the Bible; have no prayer in any form at all; until this living faith should come.[103] Wesley defined "stillness" by saying "that a man cannot attain to salvation by his own wisdom, strength, righteousness, goodness, merits, or works; that therefore, he applies to God for it. . . . and thus quietly waits for his salvation."[104]

Wesley rejected absolutely this doctrine of "stillness." He had a conversation with Molther and stated categorically his opposition. He believed it was right to go to church; to communicate; to fast; to use as much private prayer as he could; to read the Scripture. This was a definite stand against the Moravians and for the Established Church.[105] Wesley told the Moravians plainly that they violated the law of God and disobeyed Him.[106] At his early morning band meetings he took up this subject in a systematic manner and urged his followers

---
[101] *Life of Wesley*, vol. ii, p. 131.
[102] *Jour.*, vol. ii, p. 312ff.
[103] *Ibid.*, vol. ii, p. 344.
[104] *Ibid.*, vol. iii, p. 258.
[105] *Ibid.*, vol. ii, p. 330.
[106] *Works*, vol. vi, p. 23.

to obey the ordinances of God. He claimed that God commanded men to search the Scriptures. He asserted that the Lord's Supper was a means of grace and that no grace could be obtained unless one partook of it. No sense of fitness was required, but only a sense of unworthiness.[107] With such opinions as these there could be no harmony between Wesley and the Moravians.

July 16, 1740, there was a debate lasting until eleven o'clock at night with the Moravians of Fetter Lane. At its conclusion Wesley remarked, "this place is taken for the Germans."[108] But there was no decision reached; for a few days later he declared that Moravian assertions were contrary to the Word of God. He called upon all who agreed with him to leave Fetter Lane. About eighteen or so followed him.[109] These followers from Fetter Lane met at the Foundry and there organized on July 23, 1740.[110]

The separation from the Moravians was now complete. Wesley seemed to have seen his danger. He accused the Moravians of leaning on the authority of modern mysticism.[111] He felt that the Moravians were a menace to the Church, because they prevented people from attending the Church.[112]

Because Wesley had visited the Moravians and learned their tenets, it was assumed by writers of the Church that he was one of them. This hurt Methodism; so when he broke with the Moravians this opinion had to give way.[113] And people did not think well of the Moravians. Henry Rimus pictured them in an extensive narrative as being fanciful and full of mysticism.[114] Bishop Gibson said that the Moravians decried all moral law as not being a part of Christianity; all human qualifications for the ministry; all human helps toward the conversion and conviction of sinners. He concluded that the Methodists

---

[107] *Jour.*, vol. ii, pp. 356-362.
[108] *Ibid.*, vol. ii, p. 368.
[109] *Ibid.*, vol. ii, p. 370.
[110] *Ibid.*, vol. ii, p. 371.
[111] *Ibid.*, vol. ii, p. 490ff.
[112] *Ibid.*, vol. iii, p. 176.
[113] Evans: p. 109.
[114] *Candid Narrative, passim.*

went to learn these opinions.[115] Now that the Methodists had left the Moravians they could not be accused of indulging in mysticism. Wesley hereafter was very careful to keep his skirts clear from any form of mysticism. When a very old man, he wrote a letter to Mr. Walter Churchey, and mentioning his brother's hymns, said, "Those of them that savour a little of mysticism I have rather corrected or expunged." [116]

Thus have we seen the cordial dislike of the clergy and Church for any form of enthusiasm. The Methodists were classed as enthusiasts. The fact that they ejected forms of enthusiasm from their midst, as in the case of the French Prophets, Thomas Maxfield, George Bell, and the mysticism of the Moravians; the fact that they kept their movement comparatively free from such fanaticism seemed not to be maturely considered by the clergy. They were enthusiasts, and that was an end to it. The two groups, the Methodists and the Churchmen, had two radically different points of view. Their ideas of religion were different. So long as they remained so both groups could not remain in the Established Church at the same time. Either the Church must be disrupted, or else one group must leave it. The latter happened.

---

[115] *Observations Upon the Conduct of Methodists*, p. 7.
[116] Letters in *Works*, vol. vii, p. 87.

CHAPTER III

METHODIST DOCTRINE

We have seen that the outlook of the Methodists in the eighteenth century was peculiar. They saw the world around them hastening to destruction, and heard the insistent call to save men from the wrath to come. Their theology and doctrine, therefore, were neither allegorical nor speculative, but entirely practical. Indeed, when Jacob Behmen treated the Lord's Prayer in a highly allegorical manner, John Wesley denounced his method of interpretation.[1]

Section I. Original Sin

The Methodists accounted for the evil in the world by adopting Augustine's theory of the universal corruption of human nature, generally termed *original sin*, which is distinctive of Western Theology.[2]

This concept was naturally based on the biblical narrative of the Fall through the sin of Adam.[3] Wesley saw the depravity of man in the universal presence of pain and suffering. Sin came into the world because Adam chose evil rather than good, and in accordance with the curse pronounced upon him, pain followed as a natural consequence. Sin brought suffering, as the pains of childbirth testify, and in the train of suffering came death. By the mercy of God a way of escape came through Christ; but in opposition to the prevailing Calvinism, the Methodists declared that the offered salvation was open for all to accept.[4]

This sin which came in through Adam's fall continued to grow. In Noah's time, when nations appeared such as the Egyptians, Greeks, Jews, Indians, and Asiatics, they were wicked, and Roman poetry showed the evil of the Roman people.

---
[1] *Divinity and Philosophy of Jacob Behmen, Works*, vol. v, p. 705.
[2] Bradburn: *Methodism Set Forth*, p. 7.
[3] *Ibid.*, p. 6.
[4] *Sermon, Works*, vol. ii, p. 31ff.

Mohammedans, Popish, and Protestant people were evil. Universal misery was at once the consequence and the proof of this universal corruption.[5] Sin extended over the whole earth, for Wesley declared that the people of to-day were just as depraved by nature as they were before the flood. If they were not educated; if they knew not of the grace of God, they could be likened unto animals. Wesley said, "We bear the image of the devil and tread in his steps." If one would not admit this utter proneness to evil he thought as the heathen did. If one frankly admitted this he was Christian in his thinking. To know this moral ailment was the only method of opening the way for a cure.[6]

The pleasant writings of the past about man were all wrong. To appreciate man's true position, one must say with the psalmist that he was "shapen in iniquity, and in sin did my mother conceive me."[7]

Such was Wesley's idea of original sin. He himself was loath to use the term "total depravity"; but that is just what he meant.[8] Man was utterly depraved and save for the grace of God there was no hope. He was utterly dependent upon God to get out of this corrupt state. By "being inwardly changed by the almighty operation of the spirit of God" could man be saved.[9] Wesley was thoroughgoing in his idea of original sin. To an opponent he said, "Either you or I mistake the whole of Christianity from beginning to end! Either my scheme or yours is as contrary to the scriptural as the Koran is." His whole system depended upon accepting this doctrine.[10]

The extended treatment of this doctrine was given in Wesley's *The Doctrine of Original Sin*. This is one of his masterpieces and was intended to answer in an elaborate manner Dr. John Taylor's book, *The Doctrine of Original Sin*, which was published in 1750 and had its third edition in that same year.[11]

---

[5] *Original Sin, Works*, vol. v, p. 521.
[6] *Works*, vol. i, pp. 395-399.
[7] *Ibid.*, vol. i, pp. 352-354.
[8] Stevens: *History of Methodism*, vol. ii, p. 409.
[9] *Works*, vol. v, p. 572.
[10] *Letter to John Taylor, Works*, vol. v, p. 669.
[11] *Works*, vol. v, p. 492.

Dr. Taylor wrote in a very open-minded manner not readily found in his day. He urged his readers to seek the truth above all else, and rejected the use of proof-texts.[12] Taylor dealt with this doctrine from the standpoint of a rationalist, maintaining that this doctrine had nothing to do with true religion and that true religion could stand perfect and entire without it.[13] He objected that it was injurious to the God of nature who made us, and that made possible the placing of our moral responsibility for our sins upon the shoulders of Adam instead of our own. Taylor's argument was quite anti-Wesleyan.[14] He also asserted that God had bestowed upon us "gifts and mercy, privileges and advantages, both in this and in the future world abundantly beyond the reversing of any evils we are subjected to in consequence of Adam's sin."[15]

Other objections were made to this doctrine. Some clergy objected that the term was not found in the scriptures. They reasoned that the guilt of eating the forbidden fruit could not pass beyond Adam and Eve, and that the consequences of their sin could not pass to posterity.[16] One critical churchman with quite a modern point of view stated that "persons of a certain temper and cast of mind, can see deity in no other light than that of an almighty tyrant; and love to consider their frail fellow creatures as criminals from the cradle. . . . *Exit is animi tenor in rigorem quendam torvitatemque naturæ, duram et inflexibilem; affectusque humanos adimit.*"[17] In spite of all these objections, the Methodists insisted that mankind was quite guilty, corrupt, and lost.

Section II. Justification by Faith

If the doctrine of original sin put man into such an unhappy estate, it was necessary to have some power to save him from this eternal damnation. The Methodists explained this way of escape by means of their doctrine of "justification by faith."

---
[12] Taylor: *Original Sin*, part i, *passim*.
[13] *Ibid., Op cit.,* p. 254.
[14] *Ibid.,* pp. 256-259.
[15] *Ibid.,* p. 63.
[16] *Letter from a Clergyman to One of His Parishioners,* p. 7.
[17] *Essay on Character of Meth.,* p. 57.

The whole background for the understanding of this doctrine is that of the complete fall of man.[18]

Justification by faith was no more original with the Methodists than was the doctrine of original sin. Boehm wrote of it as early as 1714 in England in a manner almost identical with that of Wesley.[19]

With the Methodists "justification" and "salvation" meant practically the same thing when used in connection with "faith." "A salvation from sin, and the consequences of sin; both were often expressed in the word, justification."[20] This salvation was an act of God the Father. It was the pardon and forgiveness of sins, and not being actually made just and righteous. That was called "sanctification."[21] Whatever else justification might mean, it meant a present salvation. One was saved from the guilt of all past sin. Being saved from guilt, one was saved from fear; being saved from fear, one was saved from the power of sin; so that he could not be overcome by it.[22] This justification came from God as a gift—"of his mere grace, bounty, or favor; his free, undeserved favor; favor altogether undeserved; man having no claim to the least of his mercies."[23] He who wished to be justified had to fulfill a condition. He had to believe on Him who justified the ungodly. This believing on a God who justified was defined as faith and this faith was the only instrument of justification or salvation.[24] This belief, then, in Christ and that through Christ one should be saved, brought justification. It was not speculation, it was not rationalism, it was what the Methodists called "a disposition of the heart," that saved man.[25] Conference defined justification as: "to be pardoned and received into God's favor; into such a state, that if we continue therein, we shall finally be saved."[26]

One form of opposition to this doctrine centered in a dis-

---

[18] *Works*, vol. i, pp. 45-46.
[19] *Doctrine of Justification*, pp. 5 and 14.
[20] *Works*, vol. i, p. 16.
[21] *Ibid.*, p. 47.
[22] *Sermon, Works*, vol. i, p. 15.
[23] *Works*, vol. i, p. 13.
[24] *Ibid.*, pp. 49-50.
[25] *Ibid.*, p. 14.
[26] *Minutes 1744, Works*, vol. v, p. 194.

cussion upon "good works." Wesley stated that "good works" done before justification did not count; but that good works done after justification might count; because they were done out of deference to Christ.[27] He also made it clear that justification by faith did not go against holiness and good works; yet he did emphatically declare that, "the blood of Christ alone saved; and not 'good works.'"[28] Bishop Gibson of London thought that this attitude was misleading. In a *Pastoral Letter of 1739* he said: "I hope that when your ministers preach to you of justification by faith alone, which is asserted in the strongest manner by our Church, they explain it in such a manner as to leave no doubt upon your minds whether good works are a condition of your being justified in the sight of God."[29] He then asserted that the Established Church believed in justification, but that it believed in good works too. Another time, Gibson asked if it was not carrying things too far when the Methodists did not allow a careful and sincere observance of moral duties to count for anything; for the insistence upon faith alone led the people to value these duties lightly, and to think that they were not a part of the Christian religion.[30] Others were not so moderate in their criticism, asserting that the preaching of faith without works by the Methodists was without any warrant in the Scripture.[31] Rev. Mr. Downes, one of the clergy, went even farther and incorrectly said, "The Methodists will have it that we may be saved by faith in Christ, without any other requisite on our part; the Scriptures make a gospel obedience and holy life a necessary condition."[32] An argument from history was brought forward in which the writer went back to the days of Cranmer and Gardiner, saying that the homily on this subject did not intend "to magnify too highly the efficacy of faith, or deprecate too much the necessity of good works."[33] The Churchmen felt that disregarding good works would lead the people to think altogether too lightly of

---

[27] *Works*, vol. i, p. 49.
[28] *Ibid.*, p. 16.
[29] *Op. cit.*, pp. 27-28.
[30] Gibson: *Obs. of Conduct of Methodists*, p. 9.
[31] Haddon Smith: *Methodistical Deceit*, p. 19.
[32] *Methodism Examined*, p. 31.
[33] *Principles and Practices of Meth.*, p. 69.

their moral duties.[34] Dr. Free urged the fact against the Methodists that they differed from St. James, who taught that faith without works was dead and produced no salvation. The Methodists said that faith alone produced a salvation that was quite alive.[35]

This difference, however, between the Churchmen and the Methodists regarding the matter of justification through faith was more seeming than real. Methodists, as will appear from their statements above, did not reject good works; even asserting that he who was justified would surely do good works. What they did insist upon was that good works did not come first; faith alone was the only means of justification. And so great was their emphasis upon the place of faith, that the clergy inferred that the Methodists took a negative attitude toward good works. There was no real difference; but only a misunderstanding between the Methodists and the Churchmen on this doctrine. By faith in Christ, and faith alone, could one be set free from his original sin and gain salvation.

SECTION III. THE NEW BIRTH

Justification was the great work that God did *for* the Methodist in forgiving him his sins while the New Birth, was the name given to the work that God did *in* the Methodist by renewing his fallen nature.[36] Justification expressed the forgiveness felt; but the new birth expressed the process of transformation which took place in his life. The new birth was based upon the doctrine of original sin. "Why must we be born again?" questioned Wesley. "Because, due to the fall we are not in the image of God and we ought to be. Every child of Adam is spiritually dead. He must be born again."[37] This experience of the new birth was indispensable for salvation. The epitaph on Berridge's grave summed up the Methodist position. It read:

> "Reader,
> Art Thou born again?
> No Salvation without a New Birth."

---

[34] Evans: *Hist. of Enthusiasm*, p. 118.
[35] Free: *Rules for the Discovery of False Prophets*, p. xiii.
[36] *Works*, vol. i, p. 399.
[37] *Ibid.*, pp. 399-401.

The concepts contrasting the *once born* man with the *twice born* man still hold a large place in modern thought. Francis W. Newman says: "God has two families of children on this earth, the *once born* and the *twice born*." These *once born* children do not see God as a strict judge; but as a kind Spirit in a beautiful world. When they approach God, there is little or no excitement, and no inward disturbance.[38] Dr. William James associates this concept of the *once born* man with the religion of healthy-mindedness, and says of it: "The advance of liberalism, so-called, in Christianity, during the past fifty years, may fairly be called a victory of healthy-mindedness within the Church over the morbidness with which the old hell-fire theology was more harmoniously related. We have now whole congregations whose preachers, far from magnifying our consciousness of sin, seem devoted rather to making little of it. They ignore, or even deny, eternal punishment, and insist on the dignity rather than on the depravity of man. They look at the continual preoccupation of the old-fashioned Christian with the salvation of his soul as something sickly and reprehensible rather than admirable."[39] This represents an idea common in our day.

But Wesley took just the opposite view. He, in part, accepted the idea of God as a strict judge; he preached a hell-fire theology; he damned the *once born* man, and would admit only the *twice born* man to the benefits of salvation. When sinners approached God, there usually was much excitement and inward disturbance. The "tyranny of the twice born" experience controlled early Methodist thinking.

How a man was born again, no Methodist ventured exactly to tell, for it was a mystical experience of which he knew only the results. His eye saw God. The evidence of the process was in the fruits which the transformed life bore. This showed whether the individual had new life from God, and without this new life, no man could see God; because no man was holy. Without this new life, no man was happy; for no wicked man could possibly

---

[38] Quoted in James: *Varieties of Religious Experience,* p. 80.
[39] William James: *Varieties of Religious Experience,* New York, 1908, p. 91.

be happy. This new birth was: "the change wrought in the soul by the Almighty Spirit of God when it was created anew in Christ Jesus; when the love of the world is changed for the love of God."[40]

The importance which the Methodists attached to this new birth, can best be measured by the retort of Wesley to those who denied its essential character; who intimated that attention to the ordinances of God and regular attendance at Church and the sacrament were more needful. To all who reasoned thus, Wesley answered, "all this will not keep you from hell, except you be born again. Go to Church twice a day; go to the Lord's Table every week; say ever so many prayers in private; hear ever so many good sermons; read ever so many good books; still you must be born again."[41] Here the new birth was put above the Church and sacraments. Some of the clergy could not understand how one could attend Church, partake of the sacrament, believe in the word, obey the commands of Christ, and still be lost unless he had the experience of the new birth.

The Churchman accused the Methodist of asserting that this new birth took place at a precise time. He who experienced the new birth could tell the exact hour of the happening, and the *Arminian Magazine* was said to be full of instances, wherein the people knew the exact time of this new birth.[42] "At such a time, and at such a particular place, they felt the spirit rush in upon them with such irresistible force, that they were immediately translated from the kingdom of Satan to the kingdom of God. This they make the mark of the new birth; and will allow none to be regenerated but such only as have felt this extraordinary operation."[43] Other Churchmen also thought that the Methodist believed himself to undergo much suffering before he experienced this new birth. "They are represented to undergo several purgations and lustrations ere the new birth is quite formed. Most of them feel as it were, a burning fire within them. . . . when this severe penance is at an end, they have the favor of

---
[40] *Sermon, Works,* vol. i, p. 404ff.
[41] *Ibid.,* p. 407.
[42] Wills: p. 77.
[43] *Meth. Deceit,* p. 7.

being told by their teachers that they are then regenerate and incorruptible." [44] This idea was flavored with enthusiasm; so the Churchman, if he disliked enthusiasm, could not be very sympathetic toward the new birth.

This new birth was sometimes pictured as supernatural. The Methodists were accused of believing in "Miraculous Conversion"; each one felt himself in duty bound to go out and preach. Wesley denied all of this, claiming that no more than one in five hundred had this call to preach. Rev. Mr. Potter of Norwich was told by him that the Methodists did not believe in miraculous conversion any more than to think that all conversion in its last analysis was miraculous.[45] Downes in *Methodism Examined* accused the Methodists of treating the subject of conversion as though all conversions were of the nature of St. Paul's and the other first converts to Christianity; and "as if the signs of it were frightful tremors of the body, and convulsions and agonies of the mind arising from a sense of original sin, and the corruption of human nature: the Scriptures set it forth as a work graciously begun and carried out by the blessed spirit in conjunction with our rational powers and faculties; and the signs of it to be a sincere and universal obedience to the laws and precepts of the gospel." [46] Here the two views of the new birth were contrasted. When the Methodist urged the new birth as a doctrine to be accepted on the basis of miracle, the Churchman very properly asserted that a doctrine could not be bolstered up with an unproved miracle. He demanded the proof and made an appeal to reason.[47] The Churchman thought of the new birth in intellectual terms; while the Methodist thought it to be a vivid religious experience in his life to which he gave the name "new birth".

Still other clergy felt that the good things which the Methodists claimed to enjoy under the influence of the new birth, were found within the Church as well as with the Methodists; so they

---

[44] Evans: *History of Enthusiasm*, p. 133,
[45] *Works*, vol. v, p. 426.
[46] P. 33.
[47] Green: *Principles and Practices of Meth.*, p. 15.

said the Methodists misapplied the term new birth for something already extant within the Church.[48]

The point, however, over which the clergy waxed warmest was the relationship of the new birth to baptism. Dr. Potter claimed that baptism was the first part of the new birth, while Wesley flatly denied that baptism was any vital part to the new birth; it was only an outward sign of new birth. The new birth itself was an inward change from unholy to holy tempers.[49] Orthodox Churchmen looked upon this as a departure from the true doctrine of baptism. They inferred that the Methodist placed his hopes of heaven upon feelings and impressions, rather than upon baptism. The idea of the new birth was contrary to the idea of baptism, when the claim was made that one could experience the new birth after baptism; for baptism itself was supposed, according to the clergy, to be a kind of new birth.[50] Bishop Gibson reminded the Methodists that in the baptismal service of the Established Church, the phrase "a death unto sin, and a new birth unto righteousness" was used.[51] He also told the people that he hoped, "when your ministers preach to you doctrines of regeneration or being born again of the spirit, as laid down in the New Testament; they do not tell you it must be instantaneous, or inwardly felt at the very time. . . . Life is affected by degrees."[52] Another writer brought forward the argument that a child could receive the Holy Spirit at baptism, and yet not know of it. Hence the claim for the immediate power and communion of the Holy Spirit was a "mere senseless, enthusiastic notion." This held true of the adult as well as the child and immediate communion was not needful for regeneration. Obedience to the Scripture would work this. Therefore the administration of sacrament, and no mere notion of immediate communication, regenerated men.[53] Now the Methodists were thought to deny that baptism coincided with regeneration,

---

[48] *The Question*, p. 26.
[49] *Works*, vol. v, p. 424.
[50] Wills: p. 19.
[51] *Pastoral Letter, 1739*, p. 13.
[52] *Ibid.*, p. 2.
[53] Roe: p. 8ff.

or that it consists in reformation.[54] This idea of theirs came not from the Bible, but from the Quakers.[55] To hold the doctrine of original sin, and still to deny the efficacy of baptism made perplexing work in Methodist theology for the Churchman.[56] Wesley dismissed all of these arguments as "High Church", and still insisted that the new birth was the real essential.[57]

The question of baptismal regeneration did not come prominently into the foreground at the time of the English Reformation. Neither was the Westminster Confession thoroughgoing when it said that in baptism were conferred "ingrafting into Christ, regeneration, and remission of sins." Such baptism benefited only the elect. For those not elect, it could do nothing.[58] Luther and Melanchthon held that baptism remitted both actual and original sin, and therefore all infants who were baptized and did not sin, were saved. But the English formularies left undecided the question whether the efficacy of baptism depended upon prevenient grace enabling one to have faith and repentance, in which case the sacrament was a symbol, or whether the efficacy depended upon a sacramental act. Baptism was considered necessary by all, but the precise method of its operation was not looked into. The Methodists could not view baptism in the sense of *opus operatum*, and this caused the above controversy. Had the Church made a clearer statement of this matter, this discussion could not have taken place, and she would have saved herself from the tribulations of that later and more celebrated discussion—The Gorham Case.[59]

Bishop Lavington, one of the most bitter opponents of the Methodists was more pronounced in his objections. He said that the Jesuit Nieremberg taught the new birth as did the Methodists. The Methodists claimed it to be instantaneous: so did Saint Teresa, Saint Ignatius, and others. They had the

---

[54] Wills: p. 75.
[55] *Letter from Clergyman . . . to Meth.*, p. 2.
[56] *Ibid.*, p. 6.
[57] *Jour.*, vol. iii, p. 434.
[58] Stephens and Hunt: *History of the Church of England*, vol. viii, part i, p. 319.
[59] *Ibid.*, p. 320.

same doctrine as did the Methodists. Hence this was a popish doctrine.[60]

By thus comparing the attitude of the Methodists and Churchmen toward this doctrine of the new birth, one sees not so much difference in regard to the facts dealt with, as a manifestation of two quite distinct types of mind that could not be harmonized.

Section IV. Christian Perfection

Some phase of the idea and the ideal of Christian perfection has had a place in the Christian thought of every generation. It has stood for a conception of the completeness and blessedness of the Christian experience which has attracted both orthodox and sectarian alike. "Each of the main theological systems has preserved, in the form of doctrine, experience, or tradition, one or other of the aspects of Christian perfection presented in the New Testament; but there is no consecutive history of the doctrine." Augustine admitted that perfection was possible because divine grace was irresistible. At the same time he denied that this perfection took place in this life; for the will of God appointed that sin should persist in the best of Christians to promote humility. Luther and Calvin followed Augustine in teaching that perfection is never found in this present life. Nevertheless, the Christian had the promise from God that he would finally be delivered from all sin. Beyond this, the Reformation leaders did not venture with any degree of positiveness or precision. Neither was the Church of England lucid in its statement of this doctrine. Part of the Prayerbook indicated that Christian perfection consisted in perfect love implying a cleansing from all sin; and that it was possible for all sin to die in a person in this life. The Church sought to comprehend both the Arminian and the Calvinistic views. The High Churchmen of the Nonjuror type favored the Arminian position, and since Wesley came by ancestry from this stock, he came under the influence of this teaching and held to Christian perfection from the Arminian point of view. This, in general,

---

[60] *Enthusiasm* . . . pp. 22-28.

was the ancestry of the Doctrine of Christian Perfection as held by the Methodists.[61]

After the Methodist had been pardoned by God (justification), after he had been transformed in such a manner as to be able to commune with God (regeneration), there came a third step. He who had been justified by faith, and regenerated in his life, could be purified. Such purification was called "sanctification." The doctrine of sanctification was said to be "the grand depositum which God has lodged with the people called Methodists."[62] The conference explained it "to be renewed in the image of God, in righteousness and true holiness," and faith was the instrument for accomplishing this.[63]

"To be renewed in the image of God" was a heavy claim to make. It was never brought forward very emphatically by the Methodists, for conference urged the individual to make no claim to sanctification. If any did claim this, his fellow Methodists were to do a little investigating into his life before freely accepting his claim.[64] Not many were sanctified throughout; but just before death some were made perfect in love. This did not mean that one was saved from all sin. It was "the superlative degree of justification."[65] Neither did the Methodists claim to find any concrete cases of sanctification in the Scriptures; for the modesty of the apostles, so they explained, came to the forefront. The apostles were too modest to record themselves as being sanctified, having too much sense in dealing with this subject, lest they should give the early Christians inflated heads.[66] What was sanctification? The Methodists were vague in their answer, always handling this theme very gingerly. They came to no pronounced doctrine, because that would lead to fanaticism.

Yet one part of the main doctrine of sanctification they treated in detail. This was in the form of the doctrine of "Christian Perfection."

---
[61] Frederic Platt: *Christian Perfection*, in *Hastings' Ency. of Rel. and Ethics*, vol. ix, pp. 728-733.
[62] Eayrs: p. 173.
[63] *Minutes of 1744, Works*, vol. v, p. 197.
[64] *Minutes*, vol. i, p. 38.
[65] *Ibid.*, p. 34.
[66] *Ibid.*, p. 37.

In the Conference of 1744, the first question was asked about perfection: "What is implied in being a perfect Christian?" Conference answered: "The loving God with all our heart, and mind, and soul."[67] This sounded well; but was not a clear answer, for the people asked about the doctrine of perfection so much that Wesley, in 1766, was obliged to write a treatise concerning it entitled, *A Plain Account of Christian Perfection.*[68] Josiah Tucker, no friend of the Methodists, rightly said that Wesley did not think this out alone; but borrowed from William Law, the well known mystic of that time.[69] Wesley made much more of this doctrine, however, than did Law; for even in his old age, writing to Adam Clarke, he urged that if any preacher or leader among the Methodists should speak against this doctrine they should be officers no more.[70]

Wesley spoke of perfection in a negative as well as in a positive sense. Negatively Christians were not perfect in the sense that "they are not perfect in knowledge. They are not free from ignorance, no, nor from mistake. We no more expect any man to be infallible than to be omniscient. They are not free from infirmities, such as weakness or slowness of understanding. . . . from such infirmities none are free until their spirits return to God."[71] In his *Plain Account of Christian Perfection* the subject is treated in a positive manner. By perfection "we mean one in whom is 'the mind which was in Christ,' and who so 'walketh as Christ also walketh.' . . . In a word, he doeth 'the will of God on earth as it is done in heaven.' "[72] Wesley went even farther, when he continued, "It remains, then, that Christians are saved in this world from all sin, from all unrighteousness; that they are now in such a sense perfect, as not to commit sin, as to be freed from evil thoughts and evil tempers."[73] But this, in turn, was qualified when Wesley repeatedly stated, that there was no such perfection in this life,

---

[67] *Works*, vol. vi, p. 496.
[68] *Vide* Richard Green: *The Works of John and Charles Wesley*, p. 134.
[69] *History of the Principles of Methodism*, p. 41.
[70] Tyerman: vol. iii, p. 633.
[71] *Works*, vol. vi, p. 489.
[72] *Christian Perfection, Works*, vol. vi, p. 494ff.
[73] *Works*, vol. vi, p. 490.

FROM THE CHURCH OF ENGLAND 51

as excluded involuntary transgressions resulting from ignorance, and inseparable from mortality.[74] And with this Wesley maintained that Christians were perfect in that they committed no sin. Even though the apostles committed sin, yet it was not necessary for people of Wesley's day to do the same.[75]

Wesley's treatment of this doctrine of Christian perfection was not clear either to those who came after him or to the people of his own day. Stevens, a most thorough Methodist historian, sought to clear things up by explaining, "Perfection, as defined by Wesley, is not then perfection, according to the absolute moral law: it is what he calls it, Christian Perfection: perfection according to the new moral economy introduced by the atonement, in which the heart being sanctified, fulfills the law by love, and its involuntary imperfections are provided for, by that economy, without imputation of guilt, as in the case of infancy and all irresponsible persons."[76]

Many theologians of Wesley's day did not distinguish between moral perfection and Christian perfection. The very term "perfection" as used in connection with this doctrine added to the confusion, while the Churchmen outside listened with no kind ear to the Methodists as they claimed to do the will of God here on earth as it was done in heaven; and as they claimed to be incapable of sin. They saw the Methodists to have the same human faults as themselves and so were inclined, in their misunderstanding, to look upon all Methodists claiming perfection as being hypocrites. The criticism was sharp. Rev. John Hampson, formerly a member of the Methodist Conference himself, said that perfection was no part of the possession of the primitive Christians. They made no distinction between common and perfect believers.[77] Hampson even asserted that Wesley "never could be persuaded to profess perfection himself," and that many of his preachers and people did not believe a syllable of the doctrine. And then very facetiously, he remarked

---

[74] *Ibid.*, vol. ii, p. 168.
[75] *Ibid.*, vol. vi, p. 489ff.
[76] Stevens: *Hist. of Meth.* vol. ii, p. 412.
[77] *Life of Wesley*, vol. iii, p. 55.

that "the advocates of perfection are not the most amiable people in Mr. Wesley's societies."[78]

Bishop Lavington was not so gentle with this doctrine, calling it "that summit of arrogance, a claim of unsinning perfection."[79] Evans, a clerical writer against the Methodists, thought that the Methodists were a long way from the perfection which they claimed, for they were capable of sin and did commit sin.[80]

Wesley based his doctrine of perfection upon Scripture: "According to this apostle [Peter] then; perfection is another name for universal holiness; inward and outward righteousness; holiness of life, arising from holiness of heart."[81] He bluntly said, "In conformity, therefore, both to the doctrine of Saint John and the whole tenor of the New Testament, we fix this conclusion; A Christian is so far perfect, as not to commit sin."[82]

It is here that Wesley's confusion is explained. He relied upon the apostle John for his doctrine. Now Saint John's teaching is not always consistent on this subject. John says that he that is born of God "sinneth not." He also clearly states that "whosoever sinneth hath not seen Him, neither knoweth Him."[83] John here declares, that true Christians do not sin. And yet on the other hand, he assumes that men do sin, for he provides "an advocate with the Father, Jesus Christ, the righteous," and goes on to add, one is of the devil if he loves not his brother, and is doomed to destruction; because eternal life does not abide in him.[84] Thus we have a Scriptural contradiction which in our day explains the matter a little more clearly. But in Wesley's day, no orthodox person would admit that one Scripture could contradict another. It did not enter into the thinking of Christians. When Wesley said that his doctrine of perfection was Scriptural, he was quite correct. But being correct did not take away from the doctrine any of its inconsistencies or vague-

---

[78] *Life of Wesley*, vol. iii, p. 56.
[79] *Enthusiasm Detected*, p. 146.
[80] *Hist. of Enthus.*, p. 118.
[81] *Works*, vol. ii, p. 169.
[82] *Ibid.*, vol. vi, p. 489-490.
[83] 1 John iii. 6, also iii. 9.
[84] *Ibid.*, ii. 1, also iii. 10, also iii. 15.

ness, when one realized that it was based upon a Scriptural contradiction. The doctrine presents an ideal on the one hand, and faces an actual experience in life on the other; hence its difficulty in making itself acceptable or understood.

Misunderstandings of this doctrine existed all through Wesley's life. In London, this doctrine ran to extremes. Fitchett lays the wild actions of Bell and Maxfield to it.[85] S. Parkes Cadman is of the opinion that Maxfield professed entire sanctification, and hysterical delusions resulted from it.[86]

In conclusion, one should note that Wesley never claimed perfection, that the doctrine has always caused misunderstanding and debate from the time it was first put forth until this day. Cadman seems to be within the bounds of facts when he says, "In spite of his avowals, many devout Methodists have held that while these higher levels are divinely authorized, they are not always humanly possible."[87]

SECTION V. THE WITNESS OF THE SPIRIT

Aside from the doctrines that were concerned in the Methodist scheme of salvation, such as have just been treated, there were other doctrines which gave trouble to the clergy. Among these was the doctrine of the "witness of the Spirit."

The doctrine of the "witness of the Spirit," and the doctrine of "assurance," which is a corollary to it, were treated in a modified form by Thomas Aquinas. He taught that one could ascertain whether or not one was the subject of divine grace by direct revelation from God, by one's self, by various indications. But he felt that "various indications" and "one's self" were uncertain means to this knowledge, and that direct revelation from God was very uncommon. This was practically saying that one could not know whether he had attained unto salvation or not. Luther, on the other hand, denounced the notion that the believer in Christ must remain uncertain as to whether or not he was in a state of grace or sure of salvation. Calvin, too, gave a place to this doctrine in the Reformed Church. He

---

[85] *Life of Wesley*, p. 362.
[86] *Three Religious Leaders of Oxford*, p. 344.
[87] *Ibid.*, p. 343.

linked the doctrine of religious certainty closely to his doctrine of election. Those who were elect did enjoy the knowledge of this election, and so had an assurance of salvation. The "witness of the Spirit" took on a more mystical color with the Quakers in connection with their doctrine of "the Inner Light." This "light" was the witness of God within one's self; a reliable messenger telling the believer whether or not he was saved. This doctrine, therefore, was not peculiar to the Methodists; but they gave it a new life by asserting that it was "the common privilege of all believers," and not something experienced by one man alone.[88] It was the instrument to test the validity of the whole plan of salvation: "God telling us that we are right in his sight." Every Methodist was exhorted to listen to the divine voice and to make sure that he had its approving word in his heart.[89]

From this doctrine of the witness of the Spirit, logically came the Methodist doctrine of "assurance." Assurance simply taught the Methodist that since he had received the experience of justification, regeneration, and perhaps sanctification, he might be sure of salvation; indeed, this doctrine had for its purpose, the assurance of salvation to the individual. It was the formal way of expressing the conviction which every man going through the religious experience of the Methodist type had, namely, the conviction that all was well between his God and himself.

This doctrine was attacked by many of the clergy of the Church on these grounds: The Methodist taught that a man might be in a state of salvation now, and know himself to be so. In this their thoughtful opponents agreed with them. But when the Methodist added that a man might be sure of his ultimate salvation, he was asked how this could be in view of the possibility of his falling into sin. This distinction was made between what was termed *present assurance* and *future assurance*.[90] The clergy had no sympathy with anything that seemed to them to

---

[88] J. G. Tasker: *Christian Certainty*, in *Hastings' Ency. of Rel. and Ethics*, vol. iii, p. 325ff.
[89] Stevens: vol. ii, p. 415.
[90] *The Question*, p. 29ff.

resemble the Calvinist doctrine of "the perseverance of the saints." Yet the Methodists were more opposed to this doctrine as set forth in the Canons of Dort than many of the Churchmen. The Methodists rejected any idea savoring of the Calvinist doctrine of "the perseverance of the saints," while the Church left this question an open one.[91] The attack by the clergy, however, continued.

One, in disgust with this doctrine, declared it was presumptuous for the Methodist to claim the certainty of salvation, for it filled the head with spiritual pride.[92] Another was quite incensed and called the doctrine unspiritual, quoting Saint Paul for his authority. Paul had said that we were to be saved through hope, that we were to walk by faith and not by sight; and here were these Methodists who had an assurance of the whole affair.[93] Still another said that when Paul was converted, he still continued to call himself the chief of sinners and was none too sure of his salvation; but with the Methodists "the thing is absolutely secure."[94]

Thus in this doctrine there was misunderstanding. The Methodists simply tried to phrase the conviction which they believed every saved man can and does have. The vagueness of Methodist statements of doctrine led the Churchman to read more into the phraseology of the doctrine than the Methodists put there; so he attacked it.

SECTION VI. THE EARLY METHODIST DOCTRINE OF THE CHURCH

Wesley defined the Church as "a congregation or body of people united together in the service of God."[95] More exactly he recorded: "The catholic or universal church, is all the persons in the universe, whom God hath so called out of the world, as to entitle them to the preceding character; as to be 'one body,' united by 'one spirit,' having 'one faith, one hope, one baptism; one God and father of all, who is above all, and through all,

---
[91] C. A. Beckwith: *New Schaff-Herzog Ency.*, vol. viii, p. 470.
[92] Evans: *Hist. of Enthus.*, p. 117.
[93] Kirby: p. 12ff.
[94] Scott: *Fine Picture of Meth.*, p. 23.
[95] *Works*, vol. ii, p. 154.

and in them all.' "[96] Members of the Church were composed of all those whom God had called out of the world. The building was no vital part of the Church.[97] This conception of the Church, Wesley claimed to have received from Paul, whose congregations were animated by one common hope of immortality, one faith, and one outer baptism. The National Church of England was a part of this universal Church; but was not the only true Church; rather a part of the larger unit which was the only true Church. In this Wesley declared that his account of the Church was agreeable to the Nineteenth Article of Religion of the Church of England, which stated that any Church in which the true Word of God was preached, and the sacraments were duly administered, was a part of the true Church. And still in view of this Article, Wesley plainly stated that he would include within the Church of England people who had wrong opinions, notwithstanding that the Nineteenth Article declared specifically to the contrary.[98]

In the matter of schism, Wesley was as unorthodox as in his idea of the Church. Roman Catholics defined schism as a separation from the Church of Rome, while the Churchmen defined it as a separation from the Church of England. Wesley pronounced both of these views as equally incorrect; for schism was not separation *from* the Church; but separation *in* the Church, and separation from any church according to Scripture, with or without cause, was not schism. He felt so sure of his stand in this matter, that he went to the Bible for his proof.[99] He qualified this a little, when he admitted that a causeless separation from a body of living Christians might be schism. Whether schism be with, or without, cause, it nevertheless did much harm, because in all cases of schism there must be much of hard feeling and little of love.[100]

Is schism ever justified? In answer to this question, Wesley preached, "I am now, and have been from my youth, a mem-

---
[96] *Works,* Sermon *On the Church,* p. 157.
[97] *Ibid.,* pp. 155-157.
[98] *Ibid.,* vol. ii, p. 157ff.
[99] *Ibid.,* p. 161ff.
[100] *Ibid.*

ber of the Church of England. And I have no desire nor design to separate from it, till my soul separates from my body. Yet if I was not permitted to remain therein, without omitting what God requires me to do, it would then become meet and right, and my bounden duty to separate from it without delay," and he further added, that the sin of separation would not lie upon John Wesley.[101] And yet after making such a statement as this, Wesley concluded by exhorting all to be peace makers, and to remain within the Church of England. Wesley did not believe in schism in the concrete; but clearly recognized it in the abstract. He might have been loyal in his actions toward the Church; but from the Church of England's point of view, he certainly was heretical in his thinking. It was this manner of thinking about the Church that gave him such freedom for action when the time for ordinations was ripe.

SECTION VII. THE ORTHODOXY OF EARLY METHODIST DOCTRINE

The clergy thought that much of Wesley's doctrine was heresy. Downes said that Methodism had its counterpart in any important heresy that had ever afflicted the Church, and that it could rightfully be compared with Gnosticism, Donatism, etc.[102] Richard Hill edited a very comprehensive list of statements to bring out the contrast between the various expressions made by the Methodists upon the subjects of justification, perfection, etc.[103] Wills, whose writings we have heard of, went even farther and declared that the Methodists garbled texts of Scripture, so that they might fit into their system of doctrine, to such an extent that they were quite unsound and unscientific in their treatment of the Bible.[104] And when the Methodists ventured to assert that the clergy deviated from the doctrines contained in the Articles and Homilies of the Church of England, this was pronounced an "infamous and groundless libel."[105] This unsound attitude of the Methodists toward the orthodoxy

---

[101] *Ibid.*, p. 166.
[102] *Methodism Examined*, p. 12ff.
[103] *Review of All Doctrines of J. W.*, section ii, *passim*.
[104] P. 133.
[105] Downes: *Methodism Examined*, p. 50.

of the Established Church was supposed by the clergy to be fruitful of much harm; because the Methodists "set the nearest and dearest relations at variance; disturbed the quiet of families; nay, threw whole neighborhoods and parishes into confusion."[106]

Especially strong were the clergy in their condemnation of the indwelling of the Holy Spirit which they felt the Methodists maintained. This was a principle "irrational and unscriptural."[107] "All persons who pray or preach extempore, by a pretended inward direction of the Holy Spirit, address the eternal God with an abominable lie in their mouths." There was, in the opinion of some, no such thing as the indwelling of the Holy Spirit, and to believe in the contrary was one cause of enthusiasm.[108] This attitude of the clergy toward Methodist doctrine did not change, and even the late Canon Overton held to the opinion that the new birth, guidance of the Holy Spirit, justification by faith, as preached by the Methodists, were anticlerical.[109]

Wesley's answer to these clerical attacks was to make a strong plea for an intelligent understanding of the facts of the case. He retorted to the vicious attacks of Downes, "I utterly disclaim the 'extraordinary gifts of the spirit,' and all other 'influences and operations of the Holy Ghost' than those that are common to all Christians"; and then told Downes that he was ignorant of the facts.[110] When Dr. Potter wrote that the Methodists pretended to cure the sick by inspiration, Wesley answered, "I deny that I, or any in connection with me . . . do now, or ever did, lay claim to those extraordinary operations of the spirit."[111] To Mr. Fleury, Wesley disclaimed "as he had a hundred times before, and ten times in print," that he had any inspiration not common to all real Christians; and since this gentleman insisted upon the fact that Wesley told an untruth, Wesley curtly replied, "If you should see fit to write anything more about the Methodists, I beg you would first learn

---

[106] John Free: *Sermon, 1758*, p. 37.
[107] Roe: p. 20.
[108] *Ibid.*, p. 283.
[109] *Evangelical Revival*, chap. x, *passim*.
[110] *Works*, vol. v, p. 430.
[111] *Ibid.*, p. 424.

who and what they are."[112] To Dr. Horne, of the University of Oxford, later Bishop of Norwich, he said the same thing: Horne was not justified in bringing charges of heresy against the Methodists until he found out exactly who the Methodists were and what they believed.[113]

Wesley felt that if his opponents understood his movement better, they would find him quite orthodox. He urged his societies to obey the Church in the observation of its feast days.[114] When asked whether he did not hold doctrine contrary to the Church; whether he did not make dust of her words; whether he did not bewilder the brains of weak people, Wesley emphatically answered: "No."[115] He told Mr. Howard, who had asked what the points of difference were, that there were none; that the doctrines that the Methodists preached were the doctrines of the Church as laid down in her prayers, Articles, and Homilies.[116] Of his preaching he said, "I simply described the plain old religion of the Church of England, which is now almost everywhere spoken against under the new name of Methodism."[117] Indeed, he continually thought of himself as defending the Church from those who were secretly striving to undermine it, while he declared that all who remained with him as his followers, were mostly Church of England men who loved her Articles, her liturgy, her Homilies, and her discipline, and unwillingly varied from them in any instance.[118] These only would he have about him.[119]

No doctrine was held by Wesley that he did not think to be in harmony with the liturgy, Articles, and Homilies of the Church, and he quoted from these sources with great freedom to prove his most fundamental doctrines.[120] He named nine of the Rubrics and professed to have observed them punctually even at the hazard of his life.[121] The Canons also he claimed

---

[112] *Ibid.*, vol. v, pp. 485 and 491.
[113] *Ibid.*, p. 438.
[114] *Jour.*, vol. ii, p. 257.
[115] *Works*, vol. vii, p. 402.
[116] *Jour.*, vol. ii, pp. 274-276.
[117] *Ibid.*, p. 293.
[118] *Appeal to Men of Reason, Works*, vol. v, p. 24.
[119] *Short History of Methodism*, p. 9.
[120] *Works*, vol. v, p. 34ff.
[121] *Ibid.*, p. 27.

to obey as well as any man in England. He challenged any one of the clergy to say whether or not he had read over the Canons to his congregation as required; and then stated that he himself fulfilled this law. He professed a most loyal support to all the Canons and denied breaking any. Wesley could not have gone far astray from the doctrines of the Established Church, for the Bishop of Gloucester testified that "Methodism signifies only the manner of preaching; not either an old or a new religion; it is the manner in which Mr. W. and his followers attempt to propagate the plain old religion." Wesley let this statement of the bishop stand, for it represented his position.[122] Stevens summed well Wesley's position in the words: "The theological distinction of Methodism lay not in novel tenets, but in the clearness and the power with which it illustrated and applied the established doctrines of the English Reformation; and in harmony with its own characteristic design, merely confined its teachings to such of these doctrines as related to personal or spiritual religion."[123] If this be true, then one cannot say that the Methodists became estranged from the Church on doctrinal grounds alone. To be sure, Wesley said he was put out of the churches for preaching justification by faith alone.[124] He also said that until he preached this doctrine, he was welcomed into the churches; but a pseudonymous writer, John Smith, takes Wesley to task for this, and reminded Wesley that he was forbidden to preach in the churches before the time when he claimed to have experienced the truth in the doctrine of salvation by faith.[125] Since Wesley did not deny the error of statement which Smith attributed to him, it would seem that doctrine had little to do with the Methodists leaving the churches. When it is a glory peculiar to the Methodists that there is "no other religious society under heaven which requires nothing of men in order to admission to it but a desire to save souls, not opinions—we think and let think; nor modes of worship"— when this is the attitude of a group of people, one cannot cor-

---

[122] *Letter to Bishop of Gloucester, Works,* vol. v, p. 451.
[123] *Hist. of Meth.,* vol. ii, p. 408.
[124] *Appeal to Men of Reason, Works,* vol. v, p. 23.
[125] Moore: *Life of Wesley,* vol. ii, p. 421.

rectly think that the demarcation along doctrinal lines is very clearly cut.[126]

Doctrine, then, was not a direct cause for antagonism between the groups of Methodists and Churchmen of so great an extent that they would not live together in concord. Difference of opinion on some of the facts of religion and the interpretation of those facts was abundantly and irritatingly present; but there was no huge doctrinal gap between the Church and the Methodists. Doctrine, however, did show a state of mind, and out of this certain state of mind came a type of action. It was this which drove the wedge between the clergy and the Methodists; for this action brought out a strong opposition from the Church, and this opposition worked to establish a group consciousness among the Methodists that heretofore had not existed. Doctrine alone never could have parted the Methodists from the Churchmen. Action could and did.

---

[126] Overton: *Evangelical Revival*, p. 154.

CHAPTER IV

PRACTICES OF THE EARLY METHODISTS

THERE was no fundamental difference between the Methodists and the Churchmen regarding doctrine. But in the method of applying those doctrines, and in the emphasis put upon portions of those doctrines there was a difference. The Church believed in justification by faith; but while so believing, it was not keenly alive to the fact that men were being forever lost in large numbers. The Methodists thought they faced a world quite bad, and that their chief duty was to save souls. Great vigor in applying their doctrine resulted from this attitude of mind. Their method of application, rather than the doctrine itself, caused many of the clergy for the time being to shut the Methodists out of their pulpits. In a letter dated March 7, 1745, Wesley recorded, that about seven years ago he began teaching "inward present salvation, as attainable by faith alone. For preaching this doctrine we were forbidden to preach in the churches."[1] It would appear that it was the manner Wesley adopted in preaching this doctrine, rather than the doctrine itself, that caused the ousting from the churches. He himself told of the instance, wherein a woman in Newlyn objected to his preaching by saying, "Nay, if going to Church and sacrament will not put us to heaven, I know not what will."[2] This showed that the people in the Church felt—whether they were right or wrong is not to the point—that Wesley was against the Church and the sacrament. If this was so, they thought themselves in duty bound to keep him from speaking in the Church. It was a misunderstanding; because at Epworth the people were urged by Wesley to attend the sacrament; yet the rector would not give Wesley the sacrament because he "was not fit."[3] Wesley stated that reaction of the Methodists to this misunderstand-

---

[1] *Jour.*, vol. iii, p. 167.
[2] *Ibid.*, vol. iv, p. 236.
[3] *Ibid.*, vol. iii, p. 61.

FROM THE CHURCH OF ENGLAND 63

ing and spiritual deadness in the Established Church as follows: "They still cleave to the Church which they truly love; but being generally out from her pulpits, they had no alternative but to become, what has been called, irregular. Their hearts bowed to the opprobrium."[4] This agitation with its hard feeling forced the Methodists to adopt a certain program in order to save this world that was "utterly lost."

SECTION I. EARLY FIELD-PREACHING

Finding the churches closed to him, Wesley took to outdoor preaching. It was a "sudden expedient."[5] Wesley did not anticipate this method of spreading salvation; for when he preached a second time he described it as "submitting to be more vile."[6] Whitefield had been preaching out of doors at Bristol and had invited Wesley to come and see how it worked; but Wesley could "scarce reconcile myself at first to this strange way of preaching in the fields, of which he set me an example on Sunday: having been all my life (till very lately) so tenacious of every point relating to decency and order, that I should have thought the saving of souls almost a sin if it had not been done in Church."[7] He began this procedure by preaching on the Sermon on the Mount and quoting Jesus as a precedent for field preaching.[8] Nevertheless he never really liked field preaching. Writing to an opponent he said, "I do prefer the preaching in a church when I am suffered; and yet, when I am not, the wise providence of God overrules this very circumstance for good, many coming to hear because of the uncommonness of the thing, who otherwise would not have heard at all."[9] Overton was right when he said that Wesley had a "repugnance which he had the greatest difficulty in overcoming" for field preaching.[10]

Once begun, field preaching was carried on in a thorough manner. Wesley did away with formal prayer, that he might

---
[4] Moore: *Life of Wesley*, vol. i, p. 358.
[5] *Ibid.*, p. 361.
[6] *Jour.* vol. ii, p. 172.
[7] *Ibid.*, vol. ii, p. 167.
[8] *Ibid.*, vol. ii, p. 168.
[9] *Letter to Author of Enthus. of Meth. and Papists Compared*, p. 9.
[10] *Op. cit.*, p. 17.

get down to his audience.[11] He preached in a number of places: In Durham it was in a meadow near the river side—"quite convenient."[12] At Plymouth it was in the common.[13] At Exeter half the town came to hear him in an amphitheater just outside of the castle.[14] Time and again he simply stood in the street and gave his message.[15] At Stroud he preached in the market place, while at Kinsdale he gave his sermon in the town exchange.[16] Not only in all kinds of places; but also at all hours and in all kinds of weather Wesley labored. At Wrestlingworth, he preached by moonlight.[17] In the square of Keelmen's Hospital, it was in the rain and the hail.[18] And in a hot sun where "the vehement stench of stinking fish as was ready to suffocate me, and the people roared like the waves of the sea," he performed his mission to the inhabitants of Guisborough.[19]

Wesley was encouraged in this by large audiences. At Bristol he preached to one thousand, and later in the day to fifteen hundred at Kingswood.[20] At Gloucester he told of an audience of over a thousand.[21] At Moorfields a huge audience of ten thousand was mentioned, while at Kennington on the same day twenty thousand were recorded as having heard the gospel.[22] There was no doubt much exaggeration and over estimating in connection with these figures; but the fact remains that enormous audiences must have listened to this field preaching, for oftentimes the preachers lost their voices in seeking to make themselves heard.[23]

This field preaching was not countenanced by the Church. As early as 1739 complaints were made against the Methodists for irregularity in conduct. Whitefield, especially, was a center

---

[11] *Jour.*, vol. i, p. 449.
[12] *Ibid.*, vol. iv, p. 463.
[13] *Ibid.*, vol. iii, p. 302.
[14] *Ibid.*, vol. iii, p. 87.
[15] *Ibid.*, vol. ii, p. 294.
[16] *Ibid.*, vol. iii, pp. 29 and 474.
[17] *Ibid.*, vol. iv, p. 483.
[18] *Ibid.*, vol. iii, p. 51.
[19] *Ibid.*, vol. iv, p. 465.
[20] *Ibid.*, vol. ii, p. 175ff.
[21] *Ibid.*, vol. ii, p. 242.
[22] *Ibid.*, vol. ii, p. 273.
[23] *Ibid.*, vol. ii, p. 471.

FROM THE CHURCH OF ENGLAND

for attack and was accused of preaching without a license from the bishop, thereby acting contrary to the Canons and the rules of Christianity; furthermore, he showed a great contempt for the liturgy, for the Church, and for the clergy.[24] He and others were flayed because they had broken the vows which they took at ordination. This was surely true of Whitefield; for he was not diplomatic and in many ways goaded those who did take opposite point of view from him.[25] But Wesley's actions were considered even less justifiable than Whitefield's; because he was a man of greater learning and with a cooler head. One would expect more legal actions from him.[26] In general, the Methodists were said to break the Church law, for they did not observe the Rubrics and the Canons. The Canons, so the argument ran, forbade field preaching. Yet no one designated just which part of the Church law was violated.[27] Wesley retorted that field preaching no more violated the Canons than did the habit of playing cards, which was heavily indulged in by the clergy of the period. Bishop Gibson was opposed to field preaching because it broke the Act of Toleration; for this act provided: "That no congregation or assembly for religious worship be permitted or allowed, until the place of such meeting shall be certified to the bishop of the diocese, or the archdeacon of the Archdeaconry, or to the justices of the peace at their General or Quarter Sessions."[28] The bishop claimed that this law was not lived up to. "Nor has it been known that a dissenting teacher of any denomination whatever, has thought himself warranted, under the Act of Toleration to preach in fields or streets." Methodists were not even good Dissenters.[29] Wesley did not admit this position; for he denied absolutely that anybody had a right to class the Methodists with the Dissenters; because the Methodists were not Dissenters; but rather members of the Church of England, and since they were members of the Church, the Act of Toleration did not apply to them.[30] Furthermore,

---

[24] J. Tucker: *Conduct of Whitefield*, p. 6.
[25] *Plain Address to Followers of Meth.*, p. 6.
[26] Tucker: *Op. cit.*, p. 9.
[27] *Jour.*, vol. iv, p. 120.
[28] Gee and Hardy: p. 663.
[29] *Obs. upon Conduct of Methodists*, p. 4.
[30] *Farther Appeal, Works*, vol. v, p. 81.

Wesley might have added, that the framers of the Act of Toleration never had any idea of field preaching when they put forth this statute.

Wesley would not admit that he had broken any law, or that he was in any wise disloyal to the Established Church. To those who believed him disloyal he flung back: "And would to God all who contend for the rites and ceremonies of the Church (perhaps with more zeal than meekness of wisdom) would first show their own regard for her discipline. . . ."[31] Whenever he could attend Church services he did so; and it was his habit to attend no other service if he could find one in a Church.[32] He was very particular to keep the feast days of the Church, observing a set day for thanksgiving when England gave herself over to celebrate the capture of Quebec by Wolfe.[33] Another thanksgiving day, because of the signing of the Treaty of Paris, July 29, 1784, was duly celebrated.[34] When a Public Fast was proclaimed in 1759, Wesley preached to crowded audiences.[35] A national day of prayer because of war was observed by the Methodists in 1778.[36] On a day of prayer in 1760, set aside for the enthronement of the new king, the Methodists held three separate services for the occasion.[37] The more special feast days around the time of Christmas and All Saints' Day, a festival Wesley dearly loved, were regularly kept.[38]

In spite of Wesley's profession of loyalty, the clergy considered that he was breaking Church law, cheapening religion, and hence faithless; so they did what they could to hinder his field preaching. At Upton the clergy had the bells rung; but Wesley's voice prevailed over the noise of the bells.[39] Mr. Romley would accept no offers of assistance from Wesley while at Epworth, but in the afternoon attacked the Methodists and preached a stinging sermon against Enthusiasm. It was in the

---

[31] *Jour.*, vol. ii, p. 291.
[32] *Ibid.*, vol. iii, p. 479.
[33] *Ibid.*, vol. iv, p. 360.
[34] *Ibid.*, vol. vii, p. 6.
[35] *Ibid.*, vol. iv, p. 299ff.
[36] *Ibid.*, vol. vi, p. 181.
[37] *Ibid.*, vol. iv, p. 418.
[38] *Ibid.*, vol. v., p. 236 and vol. vi, p. 7.
[39] *Ibid.*, vol. ii, p. 346.

FROM THE CHURCH OF ENGLAND 67

evening of the same day, June 6, 1742, that Wesley, having been rebuffed by the rector of his father's former parish of Epworth, went out into the parish churchyard of that place and standing upon his father's tombstone, thundered forth a sermon on the text, "The kingdom of heaven is not meat and drink; but righteousness, and peace, and joy in the Holy Ghost"; and then, evidently his wrath stirred because of this clerical opposition, he planned to remain at Epworth a few more days to promote the spirit which had been manifested at his father's grave.[40] Opposition came from many quarters. The Archbishop of Dublin would permit no preaching out of church, though Wesley talked with him about it two or three hours. Nevertheless, on that same day, Wesley preached on Marlborough Street in Dublin.[41] Many of the clergy were opposed to this field preaching because they felt it was without results, for the people did not understand half of it, or else if they did, the noise of the mob and rabble soon made them forget what they had heard.[42] But Wesley felt that just as much religion was taken in by the people who stood out of doors to hear his words, as by the people who attended Saint Paul's, where there was the "highest indecency"; for a considerable part of the congregation were accustomed to sleep during the service, or talk, look about, and not hear a word the preacher said.[43]

The laity, too, did a good deal to hinder field preaching. At first the opposition was mild. At Bath, Richard Merchant would not let Wesley preach on his land.[44] At Saint Ives, while preaching to a quiet gathering, the service was interrupted by the mayor, who ordered one to read the proclamation against riots, whereupon the meeting was soon forced to a conclusion.[45] Men took to foolish resorts to stop field preaching. They sang ballads to take the attention away from the preaching, but failed.[46] When mild measures availed little, stronger means were adopted

---

[40] *Jour.*, vol. iii, p. 19.
[41] *Ibid.*, vol. iii, p. 313.
[42] *Observation of Mr. Seagrave's Conduct*, p. 34.
[43] *Jour.*, vol. iii, p. 373.
[44] *Ibid.*, vol. ii, p. 244.
[45] *Ibid.*, vol. iii, p. 186.
[46] *Ibid.*, vol. ii, p. 213.

and a press gang broke up one service, leaving Wesley to mourn over English liberty, property rights, and the Magna Charta.[47] While preaching at Newport, "one ancient man cursed and swore and finally tried to heave a great stone at the preacher, but could not do so.[48] Others tried to disturb meetings by driving animals in among the people who listened. A herd of cows was driven among the audience at Great Gardens, but without avail.[49] One tried unsuccessfully to drive an ox at the crowd in Charles Square, but Wesley was left victor.[50] At Pensford, there was a little more success for the opposition, when a baited bull was driven into a crowd of hearers, for Wesley was knocked clean off the table from which he was preaching. He went a little ways on, however, and finished his discourse.[51] One must not suppose that Wesley always submitted to this bad usage. He tried not to be antagonistic, but whenever opportunity offered took legal steps against those who illegally opposed him.[52]

In spite of all this opposition, Wesley felt that field preaching paid. At Bath his audiences were always serious.[53] At Newcastle, a huge crowd gathered twice on a hill in the worst part of the place and seemed "to tread me under foot, out of pure love and kindness." Though some hated him; yet with many Wesley and his preachers had an undoubted popularity.[54] Men were actually saved through field preaching, and that was what Wesley desired above all else.

Wesley never felt field preaching was a mistake. Neglect of it he always condemned as a hindrance to the work.[55] Any decrease in members in any circuit, was immediately laid to the lack of field preaching in that circuit.[56] Any Methodists who would not support field preaching were cowardly or lazy.[57]

---

[47] *Jour.*, vol. ii, p. 245.
[48] *Ibid.*, vol. ii, pp. 295-296.
[49] *Ibid.*, vol. iii, p. 45.
[50] *Ibid.*, vol. ii, p. 475.
[51] *Ibid.*, vol. ii, p. 535.
[52] *Ibid.*, vol. ii, p. 523.
[53] *Ibid.*, vol. ii, p. 234.
[54] *Ibid.*, vol. iii, p. 14.
[55] *Ibid.*, vol. iv, p. 468.
[56] *Minutes*, vol. i, p. 140.
[57] *Large Minutes, Works*, vol. v, p. 212

FROM THE CHURCH OF ENGLAND

Wesley summed up his own attitude when he said, "If ever this is laid aside, I expect the whole work will gradually die away."[58] This being Wesley's own attitude, one will not be surprised to learn that between April 2, 1739, and October 7, 1790, he preached above 42,000 sermons out of doors.[59] The result of such effort can never be adequately measured; but one may be assured of this: that "the drowsy, slippered, arm-chair religion of the day became aggressive. It attacked, instead of waiting to be attacked. Open air preaching in these modern days has itself become almost a convention, but in 1739 it was a revolution."[60]

Wesley thought himself quite within his rights as a member of the Established Church, when he went into the fields to preach. On one occasion he argued with one who claimed he was an enemy of the Church, not because of doctrine, but because he preached outside of the Church. The argument lasted two hours, but Wesley could not convince his opponent.[61] Wesley judged the Established Church to be one of the established order; yet the fact that his ancestors had supported it in the past, was to him no reason that he should support it if it were in the wrong. He plainly said that had Luther used this logic there would have been no Reformation. Hence, when the Church did not give the people the gospel freely enough, Wesley felt free to deviate from it and to go into the fields to preach without becoming an enemy of the Church.[62] "At present I apprehend those, and only those, to separate from the Church, who either renounce her fundamental doctrines, or refuse to join in her public worship. And yet we have done neither."[63]

If this was Wesley's attitude, we must look upon field preaching as the acts of self-denying men "who went forth into the highways and hedges, that they might instruct the ignorant and reclaim the lost."[64] And we must presume that "the ecclesi-

---
[58] *Jour.*, vol. v, p. 79.
[59] Fitchett: p. 190.
[60] *Ibid.*, p. 168.
[61] *Jour.*, vol. ii, p. 261.
[62] *Works*, vol. vii, p. 302.
[63] *Ibid.*, vol. vii, p. 274.
[64] Jackson: *Centennial of Wesleyan Methodism*, p. 61.

astical authorities were provoked against Methodism because it violated their rule and rebuked their failure."[65]

SECTION II. EARLY IRREGULAR INDOOR PREACHING

When the Methodists broke the conventions of the day to save men, they did not stop at field preaching; but used any and every agency they could to tell men of salvation. Not only in the fields, but indoors as well they toiled.

They used public buildings frequently. Town Halls were frequently packed with hearers.[66] The court house at Cardiff, Wales, was a place extensively used.[67] At Castlebay, Ireland, Wesley preached twice in one day in the jury room.[68] The floors caved in and rested upon hogsheads of tobacco in Turner's Hall at Deptford, but Wesley continued to preach.[69]

Hospitals, theaters, and at Northampton the riding school of the Royal Horse Guards—all these places were used.[70] Of Armagh, we read: "This was the first time I ever preached in a stable, and I believe more good was done by this than by all the other sermons I have preached."[71] Small rooms in houses of all descriptions were constantly used for assemblies.

The earlier Methodists did not scruple to use Dissenting meeting-houses, if they found the churches closed to them. In Ireland a Presbyterian meeting-house was offered both by the ministers and by the elders. It was used. The trustees of an Independent meeting-house in Bolton offered the use of their house, when the opportunity to preach in the Established Church was withdrawn. Wesley preached there.[72] Of course, the bishops could not but be antagonized when they knew Wesley and his followers were to preach in places of dissent. Had Archbishop Hutton of York possessed convincing proof of this, Wesley himself said that the archbishop would have undoubtedly suspended him.[73]

---

[65] Cadman: *Op. cit.*, p. 295.
[66] *Jour.*, vol. iii, p. 62.
[67] *Ibid.*, vol. v, p. 231.
[68] *Ibid.*, vol. v, p. 506.
[69] *Ibid.*, vol. ii, p. 283.
[70] *Ibid.*, vol. iii, p. 53 and vol v, pp. 48 and 236.
[71] *Ibid.*, vol. v, p. 312.
[72] *Ibid.*, vol. vi, p. 272 and vol. vii, p. 288.
[73] Jackson: *Life of Charles Wesley*, p. 580.

FROM THE CHURCH OF ENGLAND   71

Thus the Churchmen felt the same about this indoor preaching as they did about preaching out of doors. It was hurtful to the Church, therefore they would oppose it. Mobs repeatedly attacked houses in which Methodists preached. At Chelsea wild fire was thrown into the house and the smoke was so thick that the preacher could not see the people assembled there.[74] Robert Griffeth, of Holyhead, an old man, and the owner of a house in which Methodist meetings took place, was struck down by a stone by a captain living in that place, who wished to break up the service.[75] The opposition to field preaching and irregular indoor preaching was somewhat alike in character and identical from motive.[76]

SECTION III. THE BEGINNING OF THE ITINERACY

When the Methodists saw how their efforts to preach the gospel outside of the Established Church were welcomed by the poor who came to hear them in large numbers, it was most natural that they should seek, in their earnestness, to extend these efforts as widely as possible over England. This they did by traveling far and wide. This system of travel was called the itineracy. It was organized in no formal manner. Mr. Seward of Bristol requested Wesley to go to Bristol to preach. The people at Fetter Lane, including Charles Wesley, were opposed to John Wesley's going and wrangled much over the point. At length all agreed to settle it by lot; the Bible was opened; Wesley went; the itineracy had begun.[77] Soon after this Wesley narrated: "My ordinary employment in public was as follows: Every morning I read prayers and preached at Newgate. Every evening I expound a portion of Scripture at one or more of the societies. On Monday, in the afternoon, I preached abroad near Bristol, on Tuesday, at Bath and Two-Mile hill alternately; on Wednesday, at Baptist mills; every other Thursday near Pensford; every other Friday, in another part of Kingswood; on Saturday, in the afternoon, and Sunday

---

[74] *Jour.*, vol. ii, p. 524.
[75] *Ibid.*, vol. iii, p. 461ff.
[76] *Vide* Barr: *Early Meth. Under Persecution* in this connection.
[77] *Jour.*, vol. ii, p. 157ff.

morning, in the Bowling Green. . . . on Sunday at eleven near Hanham Mount; at two at Clifton, and at five, at Rose Green."[78] With this beginning, the work spread rapidly. Wesley himself went to Ireland forty-two times in his life, and the second largest society was, for a time, in Dublin.[79] He toured through the north of England and up into Scotland many times.[80] At Kelso, in Scotland, he began his work by singing a psalm in the market place; the chief men came to hear him; but he "spared neither rich nor poor." He was surprised at himself, for it was not usual for him "to use so keen and cutting expressions."[81] And this also may explain why the Methodists did not better impress the doughty Scotchmen with their message. Wesley visited the Scilly Islands and as late as 1788 organized a society there.[82] And when he preached at Taunton, and in the places of Cornwall, his welcome was ever warm.

It is no easy task to seek to give an idea of the extent of this itineracy. Wesley's Journal would give the impression that he preached in a different town every day, and usually in not less than three places each day. A perusal of his compiled itineracy shows that he traveled 250,000 miles and preached 40,000 sermons.[83] Others besides Wesley traveled. William Grimshaw preached as often as thirty times a week, and never less than twelve.[84]

The difficulties of travel were very bad. One who knows England knows that roads at this time were beyond description. Entertainment often was equally bad. At Oxwich, Wesley recorded: "After I had stayed a while in the street (for there was no publiic house), a poor woman gave me house room. Having had nothing since breakfast, I was very willing to eat and drink; but she simply told me that she had nothing in the house but a dram of gin. However, I afterwards procured a

---

[78] *Jour.*, vol. ii, p. 198ff.
[79] Overton: *Op. cit.*, p. 114.
[80] *Jour.*, vol. iii, p. 23ff., and vol. v, p. 236.
[81] *Ibid.*, vol. iv, p. 219.
[82] *Ibid.*, vol. iii, p. 91.
[83] W. H. S. *Proceedings*, vol. vi, pp. 149ff. gives a detailed account of Wesley's itineracy and should be consulted in this connection.
[84] Overton: *Evangelical Rev.*, p. 62.

FROM THE CHURCH OF ENGLAND 73

dish of tea from another house and was much refreshed."[85] And again: "My lodging is not such as I should have chosen, but what Providence chooses is always good. My bed was considerably under ground, the room serving both for a bed chamber and a cellar. The closeness was more troublesome at first than the coolness, but I let in a little fresh air by breaking a pane of paper (put by way of glass) in the window, and then slept sound till morning."[86]

Wesley must have thought that this traveling from place to place paid, or else he would not have put up with so much hardship, or advocated the itineracy so strenuously. When there was no increase in Methodist membership, Wesley easily attributed this to the fact that "one preacher stays two or three months at a time preaching on Sunday mornings and three or four evenings a week. Can a Methodist preacher preserve either bodily health, or spiritual life with this exercise?"[87] Such was the emphasis Wesley put upon the itineracy.

If the clergy objected to field preaching, and irregular indoor preaching, of course they objected to the itineracy, which was essentially organized field preaching and irregular indoor preaching. It was with some justice that the clergy reasoned against the itineracy when they said that traveling Methodist preachers tended to make the people of a community have little esteem for their regular ministers. Ordination was limited for this very purpose; yet this itineracy tried to undo just what the bishops sought to do. Then, too, the Church had plenty of ministers and did not need these itinerants.[88] This sounded strangely like the arguments brought against the Dominicans and the Franciscans. Whitefield was accused of breaking the law—if he insisted on preaching, he should have a chance to preach to fellow-prisoners—so the critic facetiously remarked.[89] When the Bishop of Gloucester indicated that he broke the law, Whitefield defended himself and said of this opposition, "I can

---

[85] *Jour.*, vol. v, p. 90ff.
[86] *Ibid.*, vol. iv, p. 32.
[87] *Ibid.*, vol. vi, p. 19.
[88] Gibson: *Observation of Meth.*, p. 11ff.
[89] Josiah Tucker: *Account of Whitefield*, p. 4.

foresee the consequences very well. They have in one sense, already thrust us out of the synagogues. By and by, they will think it is doing God a service to kill us."[90] Wesley faced this opposition which asserted that he broke the Canons saying: "I have no parish of my own. God tells me to preach and teach. Who shall I obey, God or man?" Then he announced to the clergy his slogan, "I look upon the world as my parish." This showed no compromise.[91]

Thus was the itineracy established, and so well did it function, that the none too friendly Hampson said, "So long as the itineracy can be preserved, and a frequent change of preachers kept up, so long will Methodism prosper."[92]

Section IV. The Use of Lay Preachers

The clergy considered that the unusual practices of the Methodists in the above described forms were bad enough, and these practices at first were primarily the work of regularly trained clergy—clergymen with the same ecclesiastical standing in the Church as themselves. But in their zeal to save the world, the Methodists were willing to go to even farther extremes. They were willing to use laymen. This irregularity—irregular from the standpoint of a Churchman—nettled the clergy and the Established Church much more than the irregularities committed by the regular clergy. When Wesley used lay preachers, he was not original, for as Lelièvre said, "le ministère laïque existait déjà depuis quelques années et avait fait ses preuves."[93]

The reason for introducing lay preachers into the Methodist plan was the practical need of the day. So many people came under Wesley's care that he had to decide whether he should confine his labors to those whom he could visit constantly or within a short space of time, or whether he should obtain other assistance.[94] After Whitefield preached one day at Islington, a layman named Bowers stood upon a table and addressed the

---

[90] *Whitefield's Jour.*, p. 295ff.
[91] *Jour.*, vol. ii, p. 217ff.
[92] *Ibid.*, vol. iii, p. 74ff.
[93] *Vie de Wesley*, p. 139.
[94] Moore: *Life of Wesley*, vol. i, pp. 413-414.

crowd. Charles Wesley was so hot at the spectacle that he withdrew. Bowers was arrested at Oxford and rebuked by Charles Wesley; but his brother John saw the opportunity in the affair.[95] Shortly afterward he chose Thomas Maxfield as one of his helpers. Maxfield was Wesley's first lay preacher.

The way now opened; Wesley had many to help him. Thomas Walsh preached in Ireland with great results, came later to England and contracted tuberculosis, thus ending his life.[96] John Bennett was an able person who accompanied Wesley on many of his journeys.[97] John Jones, a physician, also came to preach for Wesley, though later he left the Methodists.[98] These men preached, traveled with Wesley, and assisted him in every way possible.

Great care was taken with the selection of these men. Wesley listened to their preaching and then examined the practical results of their efforts. It was not polity nor doctrine but practical results that counted with Wesley.[99] Yet as the work progressed, the men were carefully examined as to their orthodoxy and other abilities.[100] By the year 1765, these men were "admitted on trial," or "admitted in full," and Wesley regularly appointed them to circuits for one year.[101]

It was to be expected that among such men as were selected to be lay preachers, those would be found who were undesirable. Complaints were made against these men. Wesley on each occasion investigated these complaints. "He found one or two, who did not walk worthy of the Gospel; and several more whom they thought utterly unqualified to preach."[102] Mr. Parker must have been one of these, for he is described as "a more artless preacher I never heard."[103] Conference took up the matter of inefficient lay preachers, and intimated that many were unqualified for the work, having neither grace nor gifts; but the

---

[95] Fitchett: p. 205.
[96] *Jour.*, vol. iv, pp. 43 and 275.
[97] *Ibid.*, vol. iii, pp. 142, 375, note 1.
[98] *Jour.*, vol. iii, p. 273.
[99] Moore: *Op. cit.*, vol. i, pp. 414-415.
[100] W. H. S. *Proceedings*, vol. viii, p. 178.
[101] *Minutes*, vol. i, p. 46.
[102] Whitehead: *Life of Wesley*, vol. ii, p. 264.
[103] *Jour.*, vol. iv, p. 248.

more serious charges against lay preachers, Conference dismissed after a careful investigation as advanced without foundation.[104]

When Wesley saw the condition of the material which he had in his lay preachers, he toiled mightily to improve it. He made an agreement with Charles Wesley outlining the general principles they both would use in selecting lay preachers. He exhorted these lay preachers not to be lazy; but to continue at their regular trades, or else to devote as much time to reading as they were wont to devote to their trades. He opposed utterly a lazy or ignorant preacher.[105] Later on, Conference decided that these lay preachers must give up their work in order to study, if they would preach for the Methodists.[106] Wesley read to his preachers from the best theological works of the times to improve their minds.[107] He looked with much sympathy on John Fletcher's plan to have Kingswood used as a school to prepare ignorant preachers for ordination.[108] Nor were the little things forgotten. Alexander Coates was told not to contradict the tenets of other sects, especially when in their churches; neither was he to use strong rhetorical expressions— he was to keep out of all controversy.[109] Wesley felt that God made practical divinity necessary, and the devil made it controversial. Hence the lay preachers were to avoid all controversy they could.[110] When they prayed too long, talked too long, or preached over an hour, Wesley was sure to be heard from.[111] He kept a close watch on all their doings. Francis Wolf was told he was "out of his wits" because he neglected to come to Conference; Thomas Carlill was ordered to attend Conference from his circuit and "none other"; William Stevens was plainly told that he ought to marry; and even William Shent was not forgotten in the hardships of his old age though

---

[104] *Jour.*, vol. vi, p. 73.
[105] Whitehead: *Op. cit.*, vol. ii, p. 264ff.
[106] *Minutes,* vol. i, p. 77.
[107] *Jour.*, vol. iv, p. 192.
[108] *Ibid.*, vol. viii, p. 334.
[109] Tyerman: vol. ii, p 413ff.
[110] *Works*, vol. vii, p. 72.
[111] Tyerman: vol. ii, p. 163.

he had left the Methodists many years before because of his bad conduct. Wesley kept a careful oversight over his lay preachers.[112] If James Oddie forgot the annual collection, Wesley reminded him of it; if Joseph Taylor ventured to wear a surplice, he was plainly rebuked; if Joseph Humphreys became a trifler he heard about orthodoxy; and when Dr. John Whitehead was a little careless of the condition in which his accounts were brought to Conference, he was told to bring them in a proper manner.[113]

Wesley urged these men to read the many publications put forth by his press. Methodist publications and Methodist publications alone should be used.[114] He even edited a good tract entitled *Directions Concerning Pronunciation and Gesture*. This was to aid his lay preachers in their public speaking.[115]

Although Wesley sought in every way to improve the interests and welfare of his preachers, yet he would not stand in the least degree any opposition from them. When Alexander M'Nabe objected because Wesley brought Mr. Smyth, a regularly ordained minister, to Bristol, on the ground that the Conference appointed the preachers and not Wesley, Wesley cleared up the matter by stating in very clear terms understood by all: "the rules of our preachers were fixed by me before any Conference existed. . . . Above all, you are to preach when and where I appoint." Since M'Nabe would not submit, he was forced out of the society and Wesley remained as an autocrat.[116] John Bennett found Wesley's discipline too severe; so he left too. There was nothing else to do.[117] Wesley had, however, much difficulty in maintaining his discipline. But he would not give it up even though he was obliged to expel many lay preachers after a long time of service. He felt that the way of efficiency was discipline, and his results seemed to justify the means he used.[118]

---

[112] Eayrs: *Letters of Wesley*, pp. 225, 227, 228, 235.
[113] *Ibid.*, pp. 219, 214 221, 222.
[114] *Works*, vol. vii, p. 67.
[115] *Ibid.*, vol. vii, p. 487.
[116] *Jour.*, vol. vi, p. 262.
[117] *Ibid.*, vol. iv, p. 15, note ii.
[118] Tyerman: vol. i, pp. 459-460.

Though Wesley was careful for his own authority, and kept the ecclesiastical power in his own hands, yet he was also keen to see that the temporal wants of his preachers were looked after. This was a very real problem, for oftentimes the poverty among these lay preachers was distressing.[119] A special fund was inaugurated for the benefit of old preachers. This was raised through gifts from those preachers who traveled on the circuits and also from the people. Old, sickly preachers and their families had first claim upon this fund; then came the claims of the widows. The purpose of all this was to encourage the laymen to give up remunerative employment and go to preaching.[120] In 1765, this fund for the preachers was further organized, and Conference declared the following terms: Every widow of a preacher was to receive once and for all not more than forty pounds; every child not more than ten pounds; every superannuated preacher was not to receive less than ten pounds yearly. But if any preacher failed to contribute to this fund, or "made less than four yearly payments into it," he could not draw from it in his time of need.[121] Thus were the lay preachers systematically safeguarded.

Wesley not only encouraged laymen to preach; but he also did not discourage women from preaching. In dealing in this subject, Wesley was always guarded. At first he advised the women to pray all they cared to in public, but not to take a text or talk above five minutes at a time. "Keep as far from what is called preaching as you can" was his advice.[122] Later on when he went to Wells, a seaport town twelve miles from Fakenham, he heard Mrs. Franklin preach at the peril of her life. She was supported by another young woman of the town with whom Wesley conversed at length, "and found her very sensible."[123] When Miss Bosanquet asked if it would be proper for her to preach, Wesley concluded that it would; because she had an extraordinary call. Nevertheless, he cautiously added that he

---

[119] *Jour.*, vol. iii, p. 494.
[120] *Minutes*, vol. i, p. 45.
[121] *Ibid.*, vol. i, p. 48.
[122] Tyerman: vol. iii, p. 41.
[123] *Jour.*, vol. vi, p. 338.

could not enforce a uniform rule in every instance.[124] Thus in a careful manner, Wesley gradually became more favorable in his attitude toward preaching by the women interested in his cause. This being the trend of sentiment, one will not be surprised to read in the Minutes of the Conference of October 27, 1787: "We give the right hand of fellowship to Sally Mallett and shall have no objection to her being a preacher in our connexion, so long as she continues to preach the Methodist Doctrine and attends to our discipline." This was duly signed by Joshua Harper, but contained this footnote: "B. N. You receive this by order of Mr. Wesley and the Conference." Evidently, the Methodists quite approved of women preachers, but intended to keep them under firm control.[125] When one can realize how utterly opposed the clergy were to lay preachers, one can in some degree realize how it must have antagonized them to see women going about and acting the part of preachers. Wesley's employment of women could not work for reconciliation between the Methodists and the Church.

The opposition to the lay preachers was a constant factor of strife between the Methodists and the clergy. The lay preachers were not always diplomatic. J. Benson rebuked Dr. Tatham of Oxford, and reminded him that Jesus himself was an untaught, itinerating preacher, and that the disciples came into the same class.[126] Collin issued a pamphlet to the "higher ranks of people" and vigorously defended himself against the charges of being too young, and of being too vehement in his address to the people. He said that none should say of him that it was unsuitable of him to preach only from the Bible.[127] If the lay preachers were not always diplomatic, those who opposed them were the same. The clergy seemed utterly to fail to understand, and therefore to misjudge these men. The clergy accused them of promoting heresy within the Church because they preached "that Christians are under no obligation to observe the ten

---

[124] Tyerman: vol. iii, p. 112.
[125] W. H. S. *Proceedings*, vol. iii, p. 74.
[126] *Defence of Meth.*, p. 44.
[127] *An Address to the Higher Ranks of People in the Parish of St. Mary Hull*, p. 16.

commandments; that the Church has done all for us, and that we need therefore do nothing for ourselves."[128] One lay preacher was accused of setting a date for the end of the world. An old man who listened to this statement believed it and turned all of his cows into his corn, let his fences go, permitted his apprentice to beat himself and his wife to cleanse them from sin, and then continued to live three years longer on this earth with the Methodists.[129] If some lay preachers did put forth such ideas as these, it was not correct to judge the whole body of them as doing the same thing.

The manner of preaching adopted by some lay preachers was very disagreeable to the clergy. They were boisterous and shocking, and were said to adopt the best of their skill to alarm the imagination, "to raise a ferment in the passions, often attended with trembling and screaming in the body. . . . the preacher has his recourse to still more frightful representations; that he sees hell flames flashing in their faces; and that they are now! now! now! dropping into hell! into the bottom of hell! This boisterous method seldom or never fails to set them screaming and very often they grow distracted."[130] The clergy thought that preaching did not consist in "noise and tone, looks and gestures; in figures and mysteries; in privileges and promises."[131] This type of preaching ought to have been condemned; but it was not typical of all lay preachers. Criticism by the clergy, however, went farther than this. They accused these lay preachers of fraud; they were said to go to preaching because they were idle and conceited; they pretended to expound by inspiration. [132] Rowland Hill asked: "But who are these lay lubbers? They are Wesley's ragged legion of preaching tinkers, scavengers, draymen, and chimney sweepers. No man would do this unless he were as unprincipled as a rook."[133] Wesley did not stoop to combat such slander as this. "Let all the world judge between Mr. Hill and me" was his only answer. In verse, these

---
[128] *Letter from Clergyman to one of his Parishioners*, p. 24.
[129] Evans: *Op. cit.*, p. 128.
[130] *Ibid.*, p. 119.
[131] Grey: *Serious Address to Lay Meth.*, p. 12.
[132] Evans: *Op. cit.*, p. 116.
[133] *Works*, vol. vi., p. 198.

lay preachers were lampooned. They were compared with vermin; called "prentices from spouting clubs"; named horse-leeches, etc.[134] Now whatever else one might say of these lay preachers, the majority of them were sincere and hard workers. It was lack of vision that made the clergy fail to see their usefulness to England and to the Church. Had they been encouraged, they would have done for England what they have already done for America. Wesley claimed to forever have answered all objections when in a letter to Mr. Clark he wrote: "O Sir, what an idle thing it is for you to dispute about lay preachers! Is not a lay preacher preferable to a drunken preacher? to a cursing, swearing preacher?"[135] Yet in this time of unhappy friction, there were those who could overcome prejudice. Mr. Brackenberg, who was at first staggered at lay preachers, finally became convinced of their worth and began to preach himself.[136]

Opposition to lay preachers in thought, was most logically accompanied by opposition in action. Mr. Westell was arrested in Cornwall for preaching; and at the quarter session at Bodmin, the court declared his arrest to be contrary to all law; so he was released.[137] Methodists' opponents used impressment as a means of getting rid of lay preachers. An attempt was made at Epworth to press Richard Moss for a soldier; but it failed.[138] Thomas Maxfield actually was pressed for the navy, because he was a disturber of the public peace. At Penzance he was thrown into a dungeon; but the captain of a man-of-war would not take him; hence they were obliged to release him.[139] Thomas Beard, who was described as a quiet man, was pressed for a soldier. Not being strong, he was soon invalided, sent home, and soon after died.[140] More violent methods were adopted against other lay preachers. John Nelson was taken before the aldermen of Nottingham for making riot; but the constable was ordered to return Nelson to the house from which he was taken.[141] In

---

[134] *Methodist and Mimic*, pp. 15 and 20.
[135] *Works*, vol. vii, p. 287.
[136] *Jour.*, vol. vi, p. 115.
[137] *Ibid.*, vol. iii, p. 251.
[138] *Ibid.*, vol. iii, p. 200.
[139] *Ibid.*, vol. iii, p. 184.
[140] *Ibid.*, vol. iii, p. 141.
[141] *Ibid.*, vol. iii, p. 239ff.

Acomb, on Good Friday, while preaching, he was struck with a brick and knocked senseless. Later on, in the same day, he was jumped on.[142]

Thus the opposition continued, and it only served to strengthen the lay preachers in their convictions.[143] They fought against being licensed as Dissenters. Sometimes they were licensed as members of the Church of England; but more frequently they were licensed as Dissenters. When this was the case, they took these licenses; but still maintained they were Churchmen. According to Wesley, the greater part of them were not licensed at all.[144] This practice could not but rouse the ire of loyal Churchmen who were careful for legality.

Hence we have a distinct practice—the employment of lay preachers—coming into Methodism. Clergymen of the Church were often more ignorant than these lay preachers; so the latter gradually usurped more and more functions of the regular clergy. At Norwich, one of these preachers even ventured to baptize and administer the sacrament.[145] Hampson admitted these men were popular with the poor; though not with the rich.[146] And he also pointed out the fact that this system gave Methodism a perpetual supply of preachers. Indeed, there was a reserve list. Lelièvre held the opinion: "Ce fut l'une des innovations qui valurent à Wesley le plus de critiques de la part de tous ceux qui faisaient passer le formalisme ecclésiastique avant toute autre considération. Ils ne lui pardonnaient pas de laisser prêcher des hommes qui n'avaient pas reçu la consécration épiscopale."[147] Overton agreed with this; for he held that although field preaching was no breach of the law, yet preaching by a layman was not only a breach of the law, but also a breach of the customs of the times as well.[148] Nevertheless, Cadman forcefully concluded, "It is apparent that they not only met a national

---

[142] *Jour.*, vol. iii, p. 290.
[143] *Vide* Barr: *Op. cit.*, Chap. v for the best account of this.
[144] *Jour.*, vol. v, p. 278.
[145] Bradburn: *The Question: Are Methodists Dissenters?*, p. 11.
[146] *Op. cit.*, vol. iii, p. 79.
[147] *Op. cit.*, p. 138.
[148] *Evangelical Revival*, p. 86.

FROM THE CHURCH OF ENGLAND

emergency, but that on the whole they were the best equipped men to meet it."[149]

For good, or for ill, the practice of lay preaching came in and remained with the Methodists. The clergy opposed it. Therefore it did not make for harmony between the Methodists and the Church.

SECTION V. THE FIRST METHODIST ORDINATIONS

If the use of lay preachers worked for an estrangement between the Methodists and the Church, the Methodist practice of the rites of ordination worked even more violently to make the cleavage more pronounced. The members of the Established Church felt that episcopacy was not only the strength of the Church, but also the unifying force in the nation; hence it was jealously guarded. Archbishop Secker said: "Without maintaining that they [Dissenters] have no gospel ministers, or sacraments, or ordinances, or churches, we may apprehend—whether rightly or wrongly is not to be disputed now, but sincerely—that episcopacy is of apostolical institution, and the Scripture affords as good a proof of this as of the appointment of infant baptism and the Lord's Day."[150] Charles Daubney clearly expressed the prevailing opinion of his day when he said that the sacraments administered in the Church and by regularly ordained clergymen, were the only valid sacraments.[151] Samuel Horsley, as late as 1830, denounced those who denied the authority of priests and bishops as little better than infidels in masquerade.[152] Thomas Sikes advocated a most thoroughgoing theory of apostolic succession.[153] The Established Church was considered an institution possessed of divine grace independent of its members. This grace was bestowed through the bishops. It was in the midst of this theory of the Church that John Wesley lived and acted.

Not everyone accepted this view of the Church. The Bishop

---

[149] *Op. cit.*, p. 329.
[150] A. J. Mason: *Church of England and the Episcopacy*, p. 405.
[151] *Ibid.*, p. 422.
[152] *Ibid.*, p. 412.
[153] *Ibid.*, p. 423.

of Bangor departed from it when he said, "Sincerity is the only thing that counts." The logical conclusion of his attitude was to make Quakers, Presbyterians, Independents, as valid as Churchmen; and William Law told the bishop so.[154]

At first, Wesley accepted the usual position of the Established Church of his day. In his sermon, *On the Ministerial Office*, 1789, he declared: "I cannot prove from any part of the New Testament or from any author from the first three centuries, that the office of an evangelist gave any man the right to act as a pastor or a bishop." This sermon discusses Wesley's attitude toward his lay preachers. He insisted that these men were appointed to preach and to do nothing more. That they were ever to serve the sacrament was a thought farthest from his head, as was evidenced by the fact that when some of them baptized at Norwich, he made them promise to do so no more. He maintained that in the Established Church, "persons may be authorized to preach, yea, may be doctors of divinity. . . . who are not ordained at all, and consequently have no right to administer the Lord's Supper." When lay preachers, as Maxfield, Westell, and Richards, were received, he was careful to explain that these were received as prophets and not as priests. They were not to administer the sacraments. Indeed, there was no need of ordaining lay preachers, for they could get along without it and be effective.[155] This was the gist of the sermon.

But aside from the practical exigencies of the occasion, Wesley read two books which made him change his mind. He read Bishop Stillingfleet's *Irenicon*. The author of this book was but twenty-four years old, and later openly avowed that he did not accept the principles in it.[156] Wesley, however, did not change when once converted to Stillingfleet's early view; for he said of the episcopacy, "that it is prescribed in Scripture, I do not believe."[157] Peter King, later Lord King, a Scotch Judge, wrote the second book—*The Primitive Church*—which influenced Wesley. This work, published about 1700, came out

---

[154] A. J. Mason: *Church of England and the Episcopacy*, p. 385.
[155] *Works*, vol. ii, p. 540ff.
[156] Mason: *Op. cit.*, p. 408.
[157] Tyerman: vol. ii, p. 244.

strongly against episcopacy. After reading it, Wesley voiced his change of opinion by stating: "In spite of the vehement prejudice of my education, I was ready to believe that this was a fair and impartial draft; but if so it would follow that bishops and presbyters are essentially of one order, and that originally every Christian congregation was a Church independent of all others."[158] In 1745, he wrote to a friend, that he believed it wrong to administer sacrament without ordination from a bishop.[159] And within one year Wesley and his Conference were at work denouncing this High Church rule. Hence, we are not surprised to hear him say, "When I said, 'I believe I am a spiritual bishop,' I spoke on Lord King's supposition that bishops and presbyters are essentially one order."[160] Fitchett explains the new view to which Wesley was won over as follows: "Christ was present in his Church. His grace did not trickle exclusively through some poor, little, uncertain, and solitary, human pipe; it did not depend upon the touch of a particular set of ordaining hands on certain human heads. It was Christ's direct gift to the human soul."[161] Or as President McGiffert states it: "but high churchism departs entirely from the primitive position. For in the primitive period as we have seen, the Church of Christ was not regarded as an institution possessed of divine grace independently of its members. . . . no special priest class existed endowed with sacerdotal powers not shared by Christians in general; and ordination, so far as it was employed at all, imparted no special grace, was not in the least requisite to the valid administration of the rites later known as sacraments."[162] This was substantially the view of the Church to which Wesley was converted.

One cannot suppose that the line of demarcation between Wesley's opposing views of ordination was clear cut. At first, in spite of any of his ideas, he was careful to have any of his men, who should administer the sacrament, ordained by the

---

[158] Mason: *Op. cit.*, p. 407.
[159] Tyerman: vol. i, pp. 496 and 509.
[160] *Works*, vol. vii, p. 324.
[161] Fitchett: *Op. cit.*, p. 405.
[162] *Am. Jour. of Theology*, 1902, p. 438.

regular bishops. In 1763, Thomas Maxfield was so ordained by the Bishop of Londonderry, who said to him, "Sir, I ordain you to assist that good man, that he may not work himself to death."[163]

When the bishops of the Established Church would no longer ordain for Wesley, he desired to get around the matter by having a certain bishop, named Erasmus, of the Greek Church, ordain some helpers for him. The Greek Bishop did this for Wesley, but it was not repeated because of discontent.[164] Lawrence Coughlan, an Irish preacher so ordained, later was ordained by the Bishop of London, and sent to Newfoundland as a missionary.[165] Dr. Thomas Rutherford was much provoked at this, and said the Methodists pretended to be loyal sons of the Church, and yet acted contrary to such a belief.[166] Neither did the Countess of Huntingdon approve of this; she suspected that Erasmus was some kind of fraud.[167] Taken all in all, Wesley did not do a wise thing in employing the services of this Greek Bishop. It was undoubtedly a *via media* policy; and as such satisfied no one. It made Wesley appear inconsistent. He frankly admitted the fact, and declared that this, his principle, was twofold: (a) he would not separate from the Church, yet (b) he would vary from it.[168] This explanation undoubtedly satisfied nobody save Wesley himself.

The ordinations by Bishop Erasmus did not allay the desire of the Methodists for more preachers who would give them the sacraments. In 1775, Joseph Benson urged that it would be a benefit to young preachers if John and Charles Wesley, together with Fletcher, should lay hands upon them after they had fasted and prayed. But in making this suggestion, Benson did not once use the term "ordination."[169] In 1782, Wesley "set apart" Adam Clarke and Cownly by the laying on of hands. These were set apart only to preach, and not to administer sacraments.

---
[163] Overton: *Life of Wesley*, p. 163.
[164] Lecky: *Hist. of Eng. in 18th Century*, vol. ii, p. 688.
[165] *Jour.*, vol. iv, p. 297, note i.
[166] Tyerman: vol. ii, p. 490.
[167] *Life and Times of Selina, Countess of Huntingdon*, vol. i, p. 331.
[168] *Works*, vol. ii, p. 543.
[169] *Jour.*, vol. viii, p. 329.

FROM THE CHURCH OF ENGLAND 87

Indeed, they did not administer any sacrament until 1788.[170] Wesley still was hesitating. His beliefs had not ripened into action.

At length, in 1784, having with a few select friends weighed the matter thoroughly, he yielded to their judgment.[171] Wesley determined to act upon the matter by bringing into use a theory which he had held for many years, namely that there was no distinction between presbyters and bishops.[172] Hence he "set apart" Whatcoat, Vasey, and Dr. Coke, not only to preach, but also to administer the sacrament.[173] In this ceremony, Cownly and Clarke, who had the year before been set apart to preach only, aided Wesley. None of these men, however, were to administer the sacrament in England.[174] These men were to serve America—not England.[175] In 1785, Pawson, Hanby, and J. Taylor were ordained to go to Scotland. Wesley did not defend this action before the Church of England, but rather asserted that it had nothing to do with the Established Church; because the Scottish Church never had dealings with the English. He did not separate from the Scottish Church; for he had never been a member of it. Therefore, concluded Wesley, "whatever is done then, either in America or Scotland, is no separation from the Church of England."[176] Wesley was now becoming more definite in his actions of ordination; for in 1786 the ordinations were not conducted in a small room with but few around, but at the regular Conference session.[177] In 1788 the time for ordination was changed from the quiet hour of four o'clock in the morning to a more conspicuous time, such as half past ten in the morning and half past three in the afternoon. He ordained deacons one day and elders the next.[178] It was also in 1788 that Wesley first ordained a person to work on an English circuit. Previously he had ordained persons only

---

[170] W. H. S. *Proceedings*, pp. 145-146.
[171] *Jour.*, vol. vii, p. 101.
[172] *Ibid.*, vol. vii, p. 2.
[173] *Ibid.*, vol. vii, p. 15.
[174] W. H. S. *Proceedings*, vol. ix, p. 148ff.
[175] Jackson: *Life of Charles Wesley*, p. 719.
[176] *Works*, vol. vii, p. 315.
[177] *Jour.*, vol. vii, p. 119.
[178] W. H. S. *Proceedings*, vol. ix., pp. 151-152.

to work outside of England.[179] Wesley was slow and hesitating about ordaining men. It would sometimes seem as though he was reluctantly pushed into it by his followers. But once having crossed his Rubicon, there was no thought of turning back. Mr. Henderson of Pembroke asked Wesley to desist from ordaining, and sent him a list of authorities to read in connection with this action. But the erstwhile vacillating Wesley had made up his mind, and told Henderson that he had no time to go into the matter; because life was too short.[180]

But why did Wesley ordain? Was it to further antagonism between the Established Church and Methodism; to fulfill a theory that was held; or to meet a practical need? The instance of the first ordinations for America may give an answer to this query.

America had received scant attention from the Methodists or any other religious body. American Methodists had sent a request to the Conference at Leeds in 1769, whereupon the Conference had sent Richard Boardman and Joseph Pilmoor over to New York. At the same Conference fifty pounds was subscribed for the work in America.[181] Practically nothing else was done for many years after, and all the while religious affairs in America were going from bad to worse. It was with great difficulty that men were forced to go to America. It was with greater difficulty that Americans were persuaded to go to England for ordination which they could not obtain in America. And "one in five, it has been calculated, of all those who set out returned no more," because they succumbed so easily to the smallpox. The teachers whom the Established Church did send out were backed by no common bond of visible unity; had no directing head; no power to ordain; they were kept like a garrison in a foreign church. The result was what might have been foretold, "the Church languished and almost passed away."[182] The Church in America was administered by the Bishop of London; but when Gibson became bishop he found himself with-

---

[179] *Jour.*, vol. vii, p. 421, note ii.
[180] Hampson: vol. ii, p. 202.
[181] *Jour.*, vol. v, p. 330, and *Minutes*, vol. i, p. 86.
[182] Wilberforce: *History of the American Church*, p. 133.

out legal right to administer American affairs, and so the colonies were separated from all episcopal control until the crown invested Gibson with special powers for America, and when he died even this personal jurisdiction ceased.[183]

Since the bishop was so far away, conduct among the clergy became very loose. In Maryland the state had to step in and use discipline. In Virginia fearless clergymen were unpopular and easily dismissed from their churches. Only pleasing pastors were chosen to serve in parishes. "Thus on every hand the Church was weakened and the laity robbed of the sacrament."[184] Serious was the shortage of clergymen after the Revolution; indeed, so serious, that Seabury went to England to obtain consecration to the episcopal office. "After waiting for two years, his request was denied. He then applied to the Scottish bishops. . . . and from them he at length received the desired honor." Yet the Methodists had no use for Seabury.[185] The clergy of Connecticut asked for a resident bishop, but did not obtain one.[186] To think that the bishops were ignorant and did nothing in regard to the American situation would be wrong. After Dr. Berkeley had died in 1753 Bishops Butler, Sherlock, and Gibson clearly pointed out America's need; but with the state politicians it availed nothing.[187] Archbishop Secker in his will appropriated 1,000 pounds for establishing bishops in America, showing that America was not entirely forgotten.[188]

Nevertheless, Dr. A. L. Cross in his work, *The Anglican Episcopate and the American Colonies,* says regarding this policy of the Church toward the American colonies: "Except for a certain oversight in matters of political and constitutional significance, it was marked by an almost total disregard of American ecclesiastical affairs. . . ."[189] In general, little was done.

With matters in this condition, some Churchmen in America wrote to John Wesley, asking him if he would procure for them

---
[183] *Ibid.,* pp. 135-137.
[184] *Ibid.,* p. 139 et circa.
[185] Jackson: *Life of C. Wesley,* p. 718.
[186] Wilberforce: *Op. cit.,* 163.
[187] Samuel Wilberforce: *Op. cit.,* p. 157.
[188] Porteus: *Life of Secker,* p. li.
[189] *Op. cit.,* p. 137.

the ordination of a young man by one of the English bishops. They explained that they did not apply to the Society for Propagating Christian Knowledge in Foreign Parts, because they did not wish any financial aid from that fund.[190] Wesley interested himself in this matter, and persuaded a Mr. Hoskins to apply to Bishop Lowth for orders. Bishop Lowth, however, would not ordain Hoskins, because the request had not come through the above mentioned society, and because he thought there were enough men already in America.[191] Wesley was as interested in saving men in America as he was in England. He knew that there were thousands of people in America without the sacraments. The questions were: Were unordained ministers to administer the sacraments; or was an effort to be made to get enough ordained clergy to supply the need; or was Wesley to assume episcopal functions?[192] Wesley did the latter, and Curteis said: "Let anyone read Wilberforce's *History of the American Church,* and he will find it absolutely impossible to speak another harsh word of Wesley's irregular conduct in 1784." [193]

Wesley himself stated his attitude toward his ordaining in detail: "But I have refused, not only for peace sake, but because I was determined as little as possible to violate the established order of the national Church to which I belonged. But the case is widely different between England and North America. Here there are bishops who have legal jurisdiction. In America there are none. Neither any parish ministers. So that for some hundred miles together, there is none either to baptize or to administer the Lord's Supper. Here, therefore, my scruples are at an end; and I conceive myself at full liberty, as I violate no order and no man's right by appointing and sending laborers into the harvest." [194] To further emphasize this he said of his action: "I exercised that power which I am fully persuaded the great shepherd and Bishop of the Church has given me. . . . These are the steps which, not of choice, but necessity, I have slowly

---

[190] Moore: *Life of Wesley,* vol. ii, p. 233.
[191] *Works,* vol. vii, p. 230.
[192] Tyerman: vol. iii, p. 331.
[193] W. H. S. *Proceedings,* vol. ix, p. 147.
[194] Moore: *Life of Wesley,* vol. ii, pp. 273-275.

and deliberately taken. If anyone is pleased to call this separation he may."[195] So firmly was he convinced of the justice of his conduct, that he announced to all who would bring him to task: "If anyone is minded to dispute, concerning Diocesan Episcopacy, he may dispute. But I have better work."[196] Wesley ordained for no other motive than that of expediency. It was the same old story: Men needed to be saved; America needed to be saved, and he was willing to go to all lengths to see this salvation take place. He worked, not in the theoretical world of theology, but in the world of practice.

At the time when Wesley ordained Coke for work in America, it was very doubtful whether he thought of this man as ever becoming bishop. Tyerman said that Coke was ambitious, and wished it to be considered as an ordination to a bishopric.[197] Indeed, he was so ambitious that he was willing to go back into the Established Church if they would make him a bishop. Whether this was so or not, Coke himself began to speak of an episcopacy at the ordination service of Asbury, and openly advocated it.[198] He spoke of himself as a Protestant defender of the episcopacy, and referred to the Methodist superintendents as "bishops," with every qualification that those of the Church of Alexandria had.[199] Asbury evidently was a ready pupil of Coke's idea, for Wesley wrote to him in the same year he was ordained: "One instance of this, of your greatness, has given me great concern. How can you, how dare you, suffer yourself to be called a bishop? . . . Men may call me a knave or a fool; a rascal, a scoundrel, and I am content; but they shall never, by my consent, call me a bishop! For my sake, for God's sake, for Christ's sake, put a full end to this!"[200] But Asbury and Coke did not put a full end to this; they went so far as to name Cokesbury College after themselves. This drew the fire from Wesley. He wrote to Asbury: "I study to be little; you study to be great. I creep; you strut along. I

---
[195] *Of Separation from the Church, Works,* vol. vii, p. 314.
[196] *Minutes,* vol. i, p. 179ff.
[197] *Life of Wesley,* vol. iii, p. 434.
[198] Coke: *Substance of a Sermon at Asbury's Ordination,* p. 9.
[199] P. 8.
[200] Moore: *Life of Wesley,* vol. ii, pp. 285-286.

found a school; you a college! nay, and call it after your own names! O, beware!"[201] Hence one can see that Wesley intended to establish no more bishoprics in the world. Moore related that Wesley never gave sanction to the departures in America—in spite of Whitehead to the contrary—for he had seen enough of bishops and bishoprics as they were then displayed in the Established Church.[202] The religious developments in America got beyond his control.

It is only too obvious to state that the opposition which Wesley faced was very sincere and very bitter. The clergy could not forgive him for this, which they considered the greatest sin of all. Charles Wesley was especially aroused over the matter. Nothing Wesley ever said or did gave his brother so much offense as these ordinations; for Charles Wesley adhered to the principle of apostolic succession.[203] He expressed his wrath in a letter to Dr. Chandler in saying, "I can scarcely believe it, that in his eighty-second year, my old intimate friend and companion, should have assumed the episcopal character, ordained elders, consecrated a bishop, and sent him to ordain our lay preachers in America."[204] Again he wrote to his brother, John Wesley, "I am on the brink of the grave. Do not push me in and embitter my last moments. Let us not leave an indelible blot on our memory; but let us leave behind us the name and character of honest men."[205] Charles went even further and stated that John Wesley separated from the Church because he had ordained. Ordination was *ipso facto* separation.[206] Wesley stoutly denied that he had in any wise separated; for he answered all of Charles's objections with a statement of his principles: "I believe I am a spiritual overseer as much as any man in England, or in Europe, for the uninterrupted succession I know to be a fable, which no man ever did or can prove. But this does in no wise interfere with my remaining within the Church, from which I have no more desire to

---

[201] *Works*, vol. ii, p. 187.
[202] *Life of Wesley*, vol. ii, p. 279.
[203] Jackson: *Life of C. Wesley*, p. 724.
[204] *Ibid., Op. cit.*, p. 727.
[205] *Ibid.*, p. 729.
[206] *Ibid.*, p. 730.

FROM THE CHURCH OF ENGLAND

separate, that I had fifty years ago."[207] Thus Wesley stood firm in his rejection of apostolic succession.

The opposition from the Established Church was very severe. John Hampson might represent a small minority, who together with Wesley rejected the apostolic succession; but the majority believed it, and that conviction gave impetus to their pronouncements.[208] George Horne, Bishop of Norwich in 1791, calmly stated the position of the clergy on this matter when he said: "We are informed the liberties taken of late years against the ministry of the Church have terminated in an attempt to begin a spurious episcopacy in America. . . . Mr. Wesley, when questioned about this fact in his lifetime, did not deny it, but pleaded necessity to justify the measure, . . . a fatal precedent, if it should be followed. . . . and the order of all things inverted."[209] "Inasmuch as Wesley was never elected or consecrated to the episcopal office, it was impossible for him to function as a bishop, and hence there would be a capital flaw in any new church he might establish. Its bishops are not bishops, and its presbyters are not presbyters."[210] The Canons of the Church said that persons should be ordained only upon certain Sundays, and that such ordination should take place in the presence of the dean and two prebendaries, at least.[211] This Canon had been violated. Furthermore, the bishops were to examine the candidates for ordination before they could ordain them.[212] Not only the law of the Church, but the usages of the Church were felt to have been shamefully treated; for this reason Wesley was denounced. William Jones said that Wesley thought himself a "vicar general" of heaven.[213] Charles Daubney described Wesley as "a schismatic grafted upon a Protestant."[214] And because Coke carried out Wesley's idea to the limit, Whitehead named him "a felon to Methodism."[215]

---

[207] Jackson: *Life of C. Wesley*, p. 730.
[208] *Op. cit.*, vol. ii, p. 192.
[209] *Horne's Works*, vol. ii, p. 570, quoted in Mason, p. 411.
[210] Hampson: vol. ii, p. 197.
[211] *Vide* Canon 31.
[212] *Vide* Canon 35.
[213] Quoted in Mason, p. 411.
[215] Moore: vol. ii, p. 275.
[214] *Ibid.*, p. 418.

And these men were right; for Wesley did break the law of the Church. "Wesley, dit-on, ne possedant pas la charge épiscopale, ne pouvait pas la conferer. En droit canonique strict, céla était incontestable."[216] Legally, therefore, Wesley was in error; but again let it be asserted, Wesley was not concerned with Church legalism so much as he was concerned with saving men. "Whether one condemns Wesley's action depends upon the fact as to whether one believes in episcopacy *jure divino* as does the High Church, or whether one rejects this view as did Wesley. It seems as though the evidence is against the High Church theory."[217] The need of getting a certain work done, was the deciding factor with Wesley; and not an abstract High Church theory.

This was a very radical departure, and cannot be thought of as making for concord between the Methodists and the Churchmen. No presbyter could usurp the office of a bishop, and continue a member of the Church of England; for the assuming of such an office, in itself, was an offense against the primary and most distinguishing institution in the Church, and therefore an actual renunciation of the Church.[218] Wesley had struck a blow at that part of the Church which all Churchmen held most dear—the episcopacy. In spirit, at least, this made him no longer a member of the Established Church. It was not his words of loyalty, but his deeds that counted. Mason said: "It was one of the extraordinary features in the character of that great man, that he was able to persuade himself that he was a loyal and consistent Churchman throughout his long life."[219] And yet, though Wesley was quite inconsistent in his conduct, when one considers the high religious values that were at stake, and the fallacy of the doctrine of the apostolic succession, he cannot term Wesley's procedure other than "an act of as high propriety and dignity as it was of urgent necessity."[220]

Thus have we reviewed the steps taken by the Methodists

---

[216] Lelievre: *Op. cit.*, p. 426.
[217] McGiffert: *Am. Jour. of Theol.*, 1902, p. 417ff.
[218] Hampson: vol. ii, p. 203.
[219] *Op. cit.*, p. 406.
[220] Stevens: vol. ii, p. 215.

FROM THE CHURCH OF ENGLAND

to carry out the convictions that came from their doctrine. They were willing to preach out of doors; to preach indoors in places other than the Established Church; to travel all over England, so that their circuit riders knew no parish bounds; to use lay preachers; and later to ordain these lay preachers. They resorted to these practices, that vital religion might be brought to every individual in England. And still, they did not resort to a single practice to which there was not a stiff opposition from the clergy and the Churchmen. With this friction and unfriendliness constantly upon the increase, one cannot say that unity of action or spirit between the Methodists and the Churchmen was increasing. The practices of the Methodists increased the tension between the Methodists and the Established Church.

CHAPTER V

THE GROWTH OF THE EARLY METHODIST ORGANIZATION

METHODISM could not exist merely in the form of religious convictions and beliefs. It necessarily assumed a corporate form and developed institutions of its own. These contributed to keep together its adherents and to conserve its peculiar doctrines.

SECTION I. METHODIST SOCIETIES

To gain added strength in their activities of saving men, the Methodists organized themselves into religious societies. Religious societies were nothing new to England; for Josiah Woodward in his book entitled *The Account of the Rise, and Progress of Religious Societies in England,* published in 1698, tells of the work of Dr. Horneck and Mr. Smithies. These two men converted several young men and united them into societies pledged to lead holy lives. These societies ministered to the wants of the poor, tried to get positions of labor for others, and brought debtors out of prison. They also had two stewards to manage their money. Woodward testified of these societies: "It has scarce ever happened that any person who could truly be said to be of these societies hath fallen from the public communion to any sect or separation."[1] Wesley's societies were doubtless based upon these societies which had existed in the time of William and Mary, and like them, were to be strictly in communion with the Church of England.[2] When the society at Fetter Lane was first founded, it was the custom for its members to go to St. Paul's for communion, headed by Whitefield and Charles Wesley; and when two members refused to go with the others, they were disowned by the society and classed as non-members.[3]

The first society was founded in 1739, and it was called the

---
[1] Quoted in *Simon,* pp. 128-130.
[2] *Jour.,* vol. ii, p. 71, note.
[3] *Ibid.,* vol. i, p. 458, note ii.

United Society.[4] In 1741, the *United Bristol Society* was formed, and was perhaps the third so organized.[5] These societies were very humble affairs in their beginnings: the society at Oxford was started in June, 1741, at the home of a Mrs. Mears, while at Sykehouse the society began at the house of a farmer, William Holme, but later the people met in his farmyard.[6] Near Brussels in an English army camp, John Haime, William Clements, and later John Evans started a society, to which officers came to listen to the preaching and two hundred soldiers joined its membership. When the camp moved to Bruges, a small hall was hired for worship.[7] At Newcastle, Charles Wesley organized a "wild, staring, loving, society."[8] The number of little societies was not limited; there could be more than one in a place.[9]

Once begun, however, these societies rapidly increased both in extent and in membership. By 1745 Wesley comments upon the strength of the several societies at Bristol and Kingswood, for the movement was well under way.[10] At Keighly ten persons soon increased to a hundred.[11] At Colchester, within three months, a hundred and twenty persons were joined together in a society.[12] In Dublin there were about two hundred and eighty members who were very teachable.[13] While in London there were 1,950 members of the societies in the year 1743, and over 2,700 members by the year 1762.[14] Sixty Irish soldiers still spoke of God and were not ashamed, in the society at Limerick.[15] When Wesley visited Saint Ives and most of the western societies, though many statements had previously been made that Methodism was on the decline, he noted that he heard nothing of a decrease, but much of an increase.[16] At Newcastle-on-Tyne,

---
[4] W. H. S. *Proceedings*, vol. iii, p. 166ff.
[5] *Ibid.*, vol. iv, p. 92.
[6] *Jour.*, vol. ii, p. 470 and vol. iii, p. 164, note iv.
[7] *Ibid.*, vol. iii, p. 152.
[8] *Ibid.*, vol. iii, p. 50.
[9] *Ibid.*, vol. iii, p. 194.
[10] *Ibid.*, vol. iii, p. 160.
[11] *Ibid.*, vol. iii, p. 293.
[12] *Ibid.*, vol. iv., p. 289.
[13] *Ibid.*, vol. iii, p. 314.
[14] *Ibid.*, vol. ii, p. 79, and vol. iv. p. 489.
[15] *Ibid.*, vol. iii, p. 477.
[16] *Ibid.*, vol. vi, p. 170.

he had occasion to reject about fifty from the society, and yet after he had done this, there were about 800 left.[17]

So large was the attendance of the members upon the meetings of the societies, that the society rooms were scarcely ever commodious enough for the people. At Dublin many hundred attended service in the morning; but in the evening, there were far more hearers than the room could hold.[18] At Hinxworth, Wesley never saw a house so full, and the people began to understand and relish what they heard.[19] At Stanhope, so many crowded in, that the beams cracked, and the floor began to sink. One man jumped out of the window. But the sermon was preached out of doors to two or three times as many people as could be gathered in the house. As late as 1790, Wesley recorded of this same place, "no house could contain the congregation, so I stood in a broad place near the Church." [20] Again, Wesley recorded, "I could not preach abroad because of the storms; and the house would not near contain the people. However, as many crowded in as could; the rest got near the doors or windows." [21] These large gatherings made it a real burden for Wesley to serve the communion, and at Bath he was glad when Mr. Shepherd offered assistance; because the number of communicants was doubled.[22] This condition of affairs was continuous, so that in his old age after making a regular visit, Wesley said, "the concourse at Birstall, about four, was greater than ever was seen there before."[23] The people were evidently very glad to join themselves together in societies to promote their practices for saving men.

These people who met in these societies had to be housed. This was a real problem; yet Wesley set about the task of obtaining rooms or houses wherein his societies could meet regularly. At York a new meeting house was built in 1759.[24] In 1752, a

---

[17] *Jour.*, vol. iii, p. 67.
[18] *Ibid.*, vol. viii, p. 21.
[19] *Ibid.*, vol. vii, p. 486.
[20] *Ibid.*, vol. vii, p. 396, and vol. viii, p. 71.
[21] *Ibid.*, vol. vii, p. 395.
[22] *Ibid.*, vol. vii, p. 435.
[23] *Ibid.*, vol. vii, p. 384.
[24] *Ibid.*, vol. iv, p. 309.

FROM THE CHURCH OF ENGLAND

new house was provided for the flourishing society at Leeds; while at Sheffield the society grew so rapidly that they could not wait for the completion of the house; but Wesley was obliged to preach in the shell of the new house.[25] A room or "tabernacle," built by a fanatic, Macdonald, who left it and went to live in Manchester, became the first meeing house in Newcastle.[26] But this room became so hot in the summer, and even hotter in the winter, that a subscription was started for a new room; because the Methodists desired to worship in comfort.[27] On April 21, 1771, in London, a proper plate suitably engraved, together with a corner stone was fixed in position with due ceremony that strangely contrasted with the humility of former years.[28]

The task of raising suitable funds for these meeting houses was an enormous one, because nearly all of the Methodists were poor. Wesley himself was always in debt on this account. He insisted, however, on owning the land upon which the meeting house was built. He would not take a gift or a loan of land for this purpose and because of this, he frankly said that when the first stone of the house at Newcastle was laid, no one seemed to know where the money was coming from.[29] When the Foundry was repaired and a few other buildings erected, the sum total of debt was £900. This large debt was later increased.[30] The way in which the needed money was raised, was by personal solicitation and personal giving. In two or three days, the people of Bristol raised £230 towards strengthening and enlarging their meeting room.[31] At Cork, Ireland, the people gave freely; in one day ten people subscribed one hundred pounds, and in three or four days more, the sum was doubled and a piece of ground taken.[32] All of this money usually came in very small sums, for when there was a gift of three or four pounds it was usually noted. There were but few times when hundreds of pounds were con-

---

[25] *Ibid.*, vol. iv, pp. 17-18.
[26] *Ibid.*, vol. iii, p. 52 and Tyerman: vol. i, p. 392.
[27] *Ibid.*, vol. iv, p. 224.
[28] *Ibid.*, vol. vi, p. 144.
[29] *Ibid.*, vol. iii, pp. 53-56.
[30] *Ibid.*, vol. v, p. 101.
[31] *Ibid.*, vol. iii, p. 331.
[32] *Ibid.*, vol. iv., p. 44.

tributed.[33] Nevertheless, as the societies aged, they became stronger; so that in 1776, in two meetings, one thousand pounds were subscribed toward building a new Foundry. The Methodist societies were becoming financially prosperous.[34]

At the beginning of the movement of building meeting houses, the officers appointed could not raise sufficient money for carrying on the work; hence Wesley took upon himself the task of paying all debts. This he did in order that he might have full liberty to preach what he wished in these houses.[35] Wesley owned all of his chapels in his own name, with the exception of those in London. In London, City Road Chapel was the only one he owned—all the rest he leased.[36] As a result of this, Wesley was constantly in debt and it was not until 1783, when over £3,000 were taken in, that Wesley found his income to exceed his expenditures. Of this sum, he reserved thirty pounds for himself.[37] Because of this heavy responsibility, Wesley was very particular to see to it that all houses were built upon the so-called "Conference Plan". This plan gave Wesley complete jurisdiction over the preachers who were to preach and the people could not oust them, provided Wesley did not wish it. In 1788, the Conference officially ratified this plan.[38] One year later, conference became even more exact and stated that no house should be begun without a majority of the building committee consenting, "and not a stone laid until the house is settled on the Methodist form verbatim. N. B. No lawyer is to altar one line." The idea was to prevent new buildings from being erected until at least two thirds of the money was first raised for their payment, and to give Conference perfect freedom to send what preachers it would to the various houses without the interference of people who did not happen to like what the preachers said.[39] The financial phase of the Methodist societies was be-

---

[33] *Jour.*, vol. v, p. 407.
[34] *Ibid.*, vol. vi, p. 117.
[35] *Ibid.*, vol. ii, p. 197.
[36] *Ibid.*, vol. vi, p. 216, note i.
[37] *Ibid.*, vol. vi, p. 392.
[38] *Minutes*, vol. i, p. 209.
[39] *Ibid.*, vol. i, p. 233.

coming an important factor in the development of Methodist organization.

The purpose of organization was to promote Methodist discipline or practices. Wesley met his societies very regularly and was exact in his discipline. If they would not attend their class, be constant at the Church services and the communion, he would not have them in his society.[40] All of the rules were to be observed—not a part only—and if a woman wore ruffles or a high crowned hat, Wesley took means to see that she put these things off, or that she be ejected from the society.[41] At Norwich, there were three rules enforced at every meeting of the society.

1. Each member must show his ticket.
2. Men and women must sit apart.
3. No spectators in the gallery during the communion.

Wesley occasionally read over all of his rules to his individual societies, stating that all who were willing to abide by them could remain within the society, and all who could not, were obliged to leave.[42] Frankness itself was Wesley's strength in this matter. "I met the society at seven, and told them in plain terms that they were the most ignorant, self-conceited, self-willed, fickle, untractable, disorderly, disjointed society that I knew in the three kingdoms."[43] This was real discipline.

Wesley not only examined the societies as a whole, but also the individual members. At Manchester he spent three days and had a private conversation with each member.[44] There was much scandal concerning the moral state at Kingswood. Wesley investigated the societies of this place and found that two persons had lapsed into drunkenness in the last three months. These were promptly expelled, but there was little reason for scandal.[45] One especial habit caused Wesley much trouble—smuggling. It was the general practice of many good people; but Wesley thought it wrong. Though perhaps in the minority, Wesley took an emphatic stand against this custom. He told the people of

---
[40] *Jour.*, vol. vi, p. 50.
[41] Tyerman: vol. iii, p. 277.
[42] *Jour.*, vol. iii, p. 68, and vol. iv, p. 304.
[43] *Ibid.*, vol. iv, p. 351.
[44] *Ibid.*, vol. iv, p. 15.
[45] *Ibid.*, vol. iii, p. 380.

102 THE SEPARATION OF THE METHODISTS

Cornwall that they "should never see his face again" if they kept up this custom.[46] At Sunderland, he waged a hot fight against smuggling and put many out of the society for this cause. Yet 250 were left. But returning there later in 1759, he reported that most smugglers had left the society and honest people had filled in the gap.[47] At Norwich he consulted with the class leaders and then asserted that discipline should be enforced if only fifty remained in the society.[48] He examined the society at Bristol and left out every careless person, and every one who wilfully and obstinately refused to meet his brethren weekly.[49] Wesley felt that this procedure was worth while. At Sutherland, he was of the opinion that one of the strongest societies existed; they scrupled even to buy or sell milk on Sunday.[50] The result of such strict standards was either to drive people unsympathetic with Methodism out of the societies, or else to strengthen their zeal and increase their loyalty. The latter usually happened. Whatever else one may conclude, one cannot deny that good members of the societies carried out Methodist practices, and Methodist practices alone.

When Wesley first started the organization of his societies he ascertained the attitude of the bishops toward them. He found that very few opposed them and that Archbishop Secker countenanced them.[51] At the same time Wesley had an interview with Dr. Gibson, Bishop of London. Both Charles Wesley and John asked him: "Are religious societies conventicles?" The bishop answered: "No; I think not; however, you can read the acts and laws as well as I; I determine nothing."[52] This did not long remain the attitude of the clergy; for soon they began to attack this organizing of Methodists into societies as being unfriendly to the Church. To the accusation that these societies divided people from the Church, Wesley responded, "if any member of the Church does thus divide from, or leave it, he hath

---
[46] *Jour.*, vol. iv, p. 76.
[47] *Ibid.*, vol. iv, pp. 220 and 325.
[48] *Ibid.*, vol. iv, p. 50.
[49] *Ibid.*, vol. iii, p. 380.
[50] *Ibid.*, vol. iv, p. 24.
[51] *Ibid.*, vol. ii, p. 194.
[52] Moore: vol. i, p. 345.

no more place among us." [53] To the accusation: you make schism, Wesley replied: "If you mean dividing Christians from Christians, and so destroying Christian fellowship, it is not. If you mean gathering people out of buildings called churches, it is." [54] In spite of these many explanations the opposition continued; for it was thought that the Methodists held too many meetings; if they held fewer, the people could devote more time to earning their living and taking care of their families, and the preachers also would be less exhausted because of too many meetings.[55] Some spoke of Wesley's societies as critics recently spoke of the Salvation Army. The establishing of his societies was spoken of as the "opening of Wesley's Mission," and doubtless many felt the same antipathy toward them as many to-day feel toward the Salvation Army.[56] Yet Wesley would not admit these charges. A society was nothing else than "a company of men having the form and seeking the power of godliness, united in order to pray together, to receive the word of exhortation, to watch over one another in love, that they may help each other to work out their salvation": this was in no sense schism.[57] But in spite of opposition, the societies grew. In Dublin there were 420 members in 1752—and that was after much rioting against the Methodists.[58]

Still in spite of his avowals to the contrary, Wesley did not forward unity with the Established Church. When he said, "I spoke to the members of the society, consisting of Churchmen, Dissenters, and Papists, that were," one can well understand the feelings of the High Churchmen.[59] This kind of organization so angered a clergyman named John Free, that he went about maligning the Methodists and in a *Speech at Zion College, 1759*, he claimed that he was spit upon by the Methodists for advocating their suppression. This showed the high pitch of feelings at the time.[60]

---

[53] *Appeal to Men of Reason*, Works, vol. v, p. 28.
[54] Moore: vol. i, p. 453.
[55] Hampson: vol. iii, p. 83.
[56] Scott: *Fine Picture of Meth.*, p. 20.
[57] *Works*, vol. v, p. 190.
[58] *Jour.*, vol. iv, p. 38.
[59] *Ibid.*, vol. iv, p. 177.
[60] P. 13.

Nevertheless, Wesley continued to perfect the organization of these societies. He printed a constitution called *The Nature, Design, and Rules of the United Societies*.[61] He sought to give each Methodist a spirit of unity by explaining at society meetings the contents of the minutes of the conferences, letters from the Methodist preachers in America, etc.[62] He saw that this organization gave new converts strength and unity; and those not so united grew faint hearted.[63] For this reason, he urged all Methodists to join them, and reproached any who stayed outside of a society because it was humble in its nature. He insisted upon a public, clear-cut stand for the society, on the part of every individual Methodist. Anything less than this was not satisfactory.[64] As he said in a letter to a friend, "one thing gave me great pain; you are not in the society."[65] And when one urged Wesley to dissolve his societies; to renounce all lay assistance; to leave off field preaching; and then intimated that he would gain honorable preferment in the Church; Wesley answered such a temptation by laboring more industriously for his societies. He well knew that with well organized societies, those practices, such as field preaching, the using of lay preachers, and ordination, which were the hope of Methodism, would be protected and furthered.[66]

Section II. The Beginning of the Methodist Conferences

Further development of organization within Methodism came out of these societies. On the one hand, the societies were further divided into classes, bands, etc., on the other, they were further united into one larger group called the "Conference." Both types of these developments had for their purpose the more effective carrying out of Methodist practices.

The first Conference of the Methodists convened June 25, 1744. The place of meeting was London, and the purpose for

---

[61] *Works*, vol. v, p. 190ff.
[62] *Jour.*, vol. v, p. 350, and vol. vi, p. 301.
[63] Moore: vol. i, p. 452.
[64] *Jour.*, vol. v, p. 83ff.
[65] Eayrs: *Letters of Wesley*, p. 116.
[66] *Jour.*, vol. iii, p. 178.

the gathering was simple: many of the preachers desired the better to know how to save their own souls, and those about them. It was a very modest gathering which lasted for five days.[67] The first Conference in Ireland took place in 1752— eight years later—and on an equally humble scale.[68] Ordained men and lay preachers attended the early Conferences; but as the ordained clergy withdrew from the Methodists, Conferences tended to be made up more and more of these lay preachers. There was no hard and fast rule in the beginning. "Most of the preachers in the kingdom were present" at the Irish Conference in 1769.[69] The question was raised at the Conference of 1746 as to who were "the properest persons to be present at these Conferences." The opinion rendered, was that the preachers, earnest band-leaders, and any other "pious or judicious stranger" were proper attendants upon the Conference.[70] As late as 1778, Thomas Taylor in his diary recorded, "To-day we permitted all sorts to come into the Conference, so that we had a large company." Thus these Conferences were most democratic at the beginning, and many besides the itinerant preachers were admitted.[71]

The reason for establishing these Conferences can best be understood from a member, Henry Moore: "For some years the preachers moved round the kingdom as Mr. Wesley thought best, from time to time, without any regular plan. But he now found it necessary to divide the whole work into circuits. This plan was attended with many difficulties, and it seemed at first that the unity of the body could not be preserved, on account of the clashing interests of circuits. But a remedy was soon found for this threatening evil, viz., to summon annually a considerable number of preachers, in order to consult together concerning the affairs of the societies. The preachers thus met with him [Wesley] at their head, he termed, The Conference." [72]

---

[67] *Ibid.*, vol. iii, p. 143.
[68] *Ibid.*, vol. iv, p. 41.
[69] *Ibid.*, vol. v, p. 329.
[70] *Ibid.*, vol. iii, p. 241, note i.
[71] Quoted from Tyerman: vol. iii, p. 271.
[72] *Life of Wesley*, vol. ii, p. 34.

From this, it would appear that difficulties in administering the system of itineracy had made desirable a body to have better oversight of Methodism and conduct its fortunes more efficiently. Therefore one can say, that the purpose of the Conferences was to promote a unity of action and feeling among the Methodists. To this end the Conference undertook to supervise the circuits; it established them as definite units in 1767. In that same year the total membership of Methodism reached the number of 25,911 persons.[73] It kept oversight of the rules governing the societies; they were read over and reaffirmed yearly.[74] The members of Conference expressly agreed not to act independently of each other, but to cooperate.[75] In 1773, the Conference drew up a set of rules which were to establish more firmly this unity. These rules were: a. The members of the Conference were to be entirely consecrated to God; b. They were to preach the old Methodist doctrine; c. They were to enforce the Methodist discipline as it was in the minutes. Forty-seven preachers signed the minutes, making this spirit of cooperation a definite factor.[76]

Since the purpose of Conference was to promote efficiency and unity among the Methodists, it considered that anything directly or indirectly pertaining to Methodism, was of concern to itself. It was careful to see that the doctrines of the Church were clearly set forth and at the very first Conference, the question of "justification" was examined and set forth in detail.[77] Other Conferences discussed the problems in connection with: three orders in the Established Church; field preaching; those who took the sacraments unworthily; the purging of the "bands"; the plan for watch-night services; and the regulation of the itineracy.[78] Conference carefully looked over the young men who were proposed for preaching and outlined the discipline for itinerants.[79] It even decided matters of personal conduct, and on

---

[73] Tyerman: vol. ii, p. 608.
[74] *Jour.*, vol. iv, p. 185.
[75] *Ibid.*, vol. iv, p. 94.
[76] *Minutes*, vol. i, p. 110.
[77] *Minutes, Works*, vol. v, p. 194.
[78] *Jour.*, vol. iii, p. 302, note i.
[79] Tyerman: vol. ii, p. 305.

FROM THE CHURCH OF ENGLAND

one occasion the question was formally asked of the Conference, "Is it right to employ hairdressers on Sunday?" The answer of Conference was, "We are fully persuaded it is not"; and doubtless those Methodists who went for their Sunday morning shave, ceased, when Conference spoke against it.[80]

Not only in doctrinal matters; but also in economic affairs Conference interested itself. Again and again, financial questions were brought before the Conference, and Conference outlined the policies that were to be followed.[81] The first scheme for raising money was brought before the Conference of 1767 and involved the raising of £5000—at that time a large sum. Conference undertook it.[82] Later New York sent over an appeal for more help, and Conference decided against this appeal.[83] It also kept in mind the conduct of financial matters within each of the local societies.

It insisted that the books of each society be accurately kept, and that the wives and children of the many preachers be provided for. This was a heavy task; but the Conference, year after year attended to it as best it could.[84]

By keeping thus in close touch with the business of Methodism, the Conference was able to prevent any movement in Methodism from going to extremes. One of the efforts of Wesley in connection with his activities at Conference, was to hold this radicalism in check. He usually opened Conference with prayer, and either he or Charles Wesley preached.[85] Wesley himself did the major share of the preaching at Conference and in this way kept control of the situation.[86] He spent a fortnight in London at the time of the Conference of 1761, "guarding the preachers and the people against running into extremes on the one hand or the other." [87] These efforts were not only aimed at the preachers assembled in Conference; but also at any other Methodists

---

[80] *Minutes*, vol. i, p. 181.
[81] *Ibid.*, vol. i, p. 181.
[82] *Jour.*, vol. v, p. 227, note iii.
[83] *Ibid.*, vol. v, p. 282, note ii.
[84] *Minutes*, vol. i, p. 87.
[85] C. Wesley: *Journal*, vol. i, p. 367.
[86] *Jour.*, vol. iv, p. 175.
[87] *Ibid.*, vol. iv, p. 477.

who might live near the place where Conference met. These were often invited in to spend a day in fasting and prayer with the preachers.[88] From this, there can be no doubt but that Conference was in a large measure responsible for the sanity of procedure that usually marked early Methodism.

Conference carried the major share of the responsibility for Methodism and so claimed a certain directing power. It outlined the duties of Wesley's assistants and these men were instructed to keep the loyalty of the people firmly fixed in the Established Church.[89] The many details connected with the itineracy were reviewed by the Conference. It claimed the authority to station the preachers where it would. John Edwards, one of the preachers, wished a permanent appointment to Leeds, but this was refused him, and he was appointed to that place for six months only. When his time expired, he refused to give up his appointment and for this cause was ejected from the Methodists. Conference succeeded in this instance in supporting its claim to the absolute right to appoint its preachers.[90] But this power did not go unchallenged. The trustees of the chapel at Birstal had it in mind to elect their own preachers monthly, and all such preachers were to preach twice each Sunday before the people of Birstal. Wesley was urged to sign to this. Such a plan as this took all the power away from the Conference and vested it in a body of trustees.[91] This matter of authority was brought before the Conference and Wesley was instructed by the Conference to interview the trustees of Birstal and present to them the claim of Conference, that the said Conference alone should have the authority to appoint the preachers and conduct the affairs at Birstal.[92] Wesley did as instructed. He requested these trustees to settle their chapel on the "Methodist Plan." Only five out of nine approved of this plan; but the chapel was eventually settled upon the Methodist Plan and the centralized authority was upheld. A little later the authority of Conference was questioned

---

[88] *Jour.*, vol. iii, p. 196, also note i.
[89] *Minutes*, vol. i, p. 40.
[90] *Jour.*, vol. iv, p. 67.
[91] Tyerman: vol. iii, p. 373ff.
[92] *Jour.*, vol. vi, p. 437.

FROM THE CHURCH OF ENGLAND

by the trustees and people of Dewsbury; and not with a happy ending. The trustees of Dewsbury went farther than those of Birstal; for they claimed the right to try their own preachers and even expel them if necessary. They wished to function as accusers, juries, and executives. Conference denied that the people of Dewsbury could try and expel its preachers, and at the same time asserted its right to station whom it would at Dewsbury. When the people of the chapel would not give in, Conference abandoned the chapel, August 14, 1788, and street preaching was begun again in Dewsbury.[93] Wesley characterized the situation, saying, "I have no right in any house in England. What I claim is the right of stationing preachers. This the trustees have robbed me of in the present instance." The preachers and the people rallied and a year later £209 was raised for a new chapel at Dewsbury. Here again, after much strife, the authority of Conference, as over against that of the trustees of local meeting houses, was supreme.[94]

Out of this opposition to the authority of Conference came the Deed of Declaration. Hitherto, there had been objections to Conference, and as there was no legal "Conference," a weak side of Methodism was exposed. What property was held in trust, was held either by the two Wesleys jointly, or by local boards of trustees. This being the situation, when the Wesleys died, things might be in a very chaotic condition. After the opposition from the trustees of Birstal, Wesley determined to incorporate and legalize the Conference. He felt that: "without some authentic deed, fixing the meaning of the term, the moment I died the Conference had been nothing.[95] This deed incorporated Conference with a membership of one hundred persons.[96] Such a corporation could hold property, and have the right to station preachers, and also other guarded privileges. The deed was signed by Wesley in 1784, and enrolled in the Court of Chancery, making the Conference legal and sovereign.[97]

---

[93] Tyerman: vol. iii, pp. 553-554.
[94] *Ibid.*, vol. iii, p. 560.
[95] T. Jackson: *Life of Charles Wesley*, p. 717.
[96] *Vide Deed of Declaration*, full text in *Journal*, vol. viii, p. 335ff.
[97] *Jour.*, vol. vi, p. 481, note i.

It assured the unity of the Methodist movement and prevented the possibility of the itineracy's ceasing when Wesley died.[98]

From within the Conference itself came hot opposition. Many who had hitherto supported Wesley, objected to the passing of this undemocratic legislation. Fletcher of Madeley, Wesley's loyal supporter, worked hard for its passage, and when it was adopted several members of Conference withdrew by way of protest. Joseph Pilmoor, the preacher sent formerly to New York, John Hampsons junior and senior, and John Atlay retired from the Conference.[99] Not only within Conference but outside also, this action was opposed. William Moore left the church at Plymouth Dock and the people were quite uneasy.[100] Hampson was very angry over the discrimination shown in choosing one hundred men to be incorporated, while leaving other men equally as able and loyal out of such an incorporation. "As every itinerant had always considered himself, on his admission to travel, as a member of Conference, and as the intended selection of the one hundred was industriously concealed, not a man, except a few who were in the secret, had the least idea of what was going forward. . . . When they saw the deed, it was with great astonishment and indignation!"[101] Because Wesley succeeded in forcing this Deed of Declaration upon the Conference in spite of much opposition, many said that Conference was of little use to Methodism inasmuch as it served only the purpose of declaring and ratifying decisions that Wesley had already made.[102] But notwithstanding its humble origin, and the many attempts to oppose its will, the Conference asserted its will and became under Wesley's leadership an institution of power, cementing the Methodists together into a more compact body than before.

Did the Conference make for separation? Verbally, No, Conference declared: "What may we reasonably believe God's design in raising up the preachers called Methodists? Answer:

---

[98] Tyerman: vol. iii, p. 426.
[99] *Jour.*, vol. vii, p. 5, note iii.
[100] *Ibid.*, vol. vii, p. 54.
[101] Hampson: *Life of Wesley*, vol. ii, pp. 160-161.
[102] *Ibid.*, vol. iii, p. 86.

FROM THE CHURCH OF ENGLAND

Not to form any new sect; but to reform the nation, particularly the Church; and spread scriptural holiness over the land." [103] And at the first Conference in 1744, the members asserted and reaffirmed in quite a little detail: that Methodists were Churchmen; they will not leave the Church unless put out; they have a proper definition of Church; their preaching will be to support the Church.[104] But in spite of all these expressions of loyalty to the Church, the Methodists by action, did just the opposite. Every time they asserted the primary authority of their Conference they thereby denied any real authority of the Established Church over them. Hence one must conclude that the institution of the Conference worked for unity among the Methodists; and therefore, for a lack of unity with the Church. One will readily agree with Prof. Faulkner of Drew, when he says: "There were profound inconsistencies in Wesley's relation to the Church of England. Professing constantly undiminished love for that Church, circumstances were always driving him to acts utterly inconsistent with loyalty thereto." [105]

Section III. Methodist Classes, Bands, Stewards, Quarterly Meetings

As the Methodist societies were united into a larger unit called the Conference for the sake of furthering their practices and increasing their efficiency; even so were they divided into smaller groups for the more extensive furthering of their practices and the greater increase of their efficiency.

In a certain sense, Methodist societies were begun in 1739, but it was not until 1742 that they were divided into "classes." [106]

The immediate cause for their formation was a financial one. The members of the societies at Bristol met together to find ways and means of discharging their common debt. A suggestion was made for doing this under three heads. a. Every member of the society contribute two cents, b. the whole society be divided into companies of twelve—these were to be called

---
[103] *Works*, vol. v, p. 212.
[104] *Ibid.*, vol. v, p. 197-198.
[105] Faulkner: *The Methodists*, p. 96.
[106] Tyerman: vol. i, p. 377.

classes, c. one person was to be appointed to receive a contribution from the members of a class and give it to the stewards. Wesley quickly fell in with these suggestions, and the system of classes was inaugurated. In the first instance, it was a system to get money.[107] The more deep lying cause for the beginning of classes was the problem of supervising the large numbers of people who came under Wesley's care. He could not attend to these individually, so he organized them into small groups, and placed a leader over them who could inspect their lives in some detail.[108] "That it may be more easily discerned whether the members of our societies are working out their own salvation, they are divided into little companies called classes." [109] Wesley summed up the reasons which prompted him to organize these classes as follows: "The need of comradeship to maintain loyalty to the cause of religion, and the need of an agency to pay the debts of the society at Bristol." [110]

The division of the Methodist societies into classes was made without regard to rank or distinction.[111] The entire society was divided into these classes and every member of the society was expected to attend a class. In 1788, there were over nine hundred in the classes of Bristol, not counting those who had been lost through moving or misconduct.[112] All kinds of people were members of these classes and Wesley recorded: "I met a class of soldiers." Some of these were stalwart fellows, thus showing the popularity of the classes.[113]

Indeed, these classes were so popular with the Methodists that one was able to restrict attendance upon them by means of admission tickets. These tickets varied in size and form at the various periods of time.[114] They were probably first given out to limit admissions about 1742. After the year 1750, texts of Scripture were printed upon them for the edification of the

[107] *Jour.*, vol. ii, p. 528.
[108] *Ibid.*, vol. ii, p. 535.
[109] *Ibid.*, vol. v, p. 404.
[110] Moore: *Op. cit.*, vol. i, p. 454.
[111] *Jour.*, vol. iv, p. 304.
[112] *Ibid.*, vol. vii, p. 361.
[113] *Ibid.*, vol. iii, p. 485.
[114] *Vide* W. H. S. *Proceedings*, vol. v, p. 32, opposite, for good reproductions of these tickets.

holders.[115] These small tickets were signed by John Wesley, or by the class leader, and were good for one quarter of a year. After that, they had to be renewed, or else the holder could not attend class. It was necessary to present a ticket to be admitted to a session of the class.[116] The Methodists must have valued these classes highly, else they would not have consented to submit to such restrictions as these.

Each of these classes was in charge of a man called the "leader". At first the leader visited from house to house; but this was dropped, for it was considered easier to get the people together.[117] These men had no authority over the assistants of Wesley, and they could not eject any member from their class without the consent of either Wesley or one of his assistants. They could not displace another class leader and they had nothing to do with the temporal affairs of Methodism. The contributions which they weekly collected in their classes, they handed over to the stewards. All other money was collected by the assistant, and the leaders were not concerned with the collection.[118] These class leaders were men of importance and influence. In Dublin the class leaders insisted in a strong handed manner on conducting things their own way. Wesley finally went to Dublin and told the leaders to stay in their places. Men of less zeal and ability would not have shown this energy displayed by the leaders of Dublin.[119] Once in a while, women were permitted to be leaders. In the old book of Yarmouth, begun in the year 1785, the name "Sister Mary Sewell" appeared as a class leader. This woman was a member of the Methodist Class, and doubtless acted as a leader. But as in the case of preaching, the woman who led the class was no more the rule than the woman who preached; although both were allowed.[120]

Wesley was very careful to see that the leaders enforced the Methodist discipline in their classes; and went to considerable lengths himself to see that it was done. Class inspection Wesley

---
[115] W. H. S. *Proceedings,* vol. v, p. 32ff.
[116] *Jour.,* vol. vii, p. 61.
[117] Whitehead: vol. ii, pp. 148-149.
[118] *Jour.,* vol. v, p. 405.
[119] *Ibid.,* vol. v, p. 406.
[120] W. H. S. *Proceedings,* vol. iii, p. 74.

considered one of the important parts of his work. At Newcastle, he spent three days examining the classes.[121] He said with emphasis, that he would not give tickets to any who did not meet in their class twelve times in the quarter unless they were kept home by sickness or unavoidable business. He urged his assistants to enforce this rule and to remove all careless class leaders.[122] Wesley's attitude may be shown by his frequent allusions to this visitation, such as: "I began visiting the classes in London, and that with more exactness than ever before. After going through, I found the society contained about 2,350 members, few of whom we could discern to be triflers, and none we hope, lived in any wilful sin."[123] The discipline was so strict that many dropped out of these classes; but in their places many entered, so great was the prestige of the class system.[124]

The clergy naturally opposed the class, as they opposed everything else that was tainted with Methodism. Their opposition was based chiefly upon the fact that these classes fostered enthusiasm. "I forbear to relate the confusion, the tumult, the noise, and uproar, which at these times disgraced the order and scandalized the exercise of religious worship." This was the view of the class-meeting held by the clergy.[125] They also objected to the intimate manner used in discussing the various phases of religious experience. "In short every case is canvassed and the great physician of souls is applied to for a sovereign balm for every wound—a salve for every sore."[126] The attack, however, on the class was not as well organized or concentrated, as against other factors of Methodism.

And where the class was "thought large to speak their minds freely, many meet once a week in smaller companies, called 'bands', consisting of four or five persons, men with men, and women with women."[127] This was the purpose of even further sub-dividing the societies into bands: it was to furnish a group

---
[121] *Jour.*, vol. iii, p. 362.
[122] *Letter,* quoted in Tyerman: vol. iii, p. 215.
[123] *Jour.*, vol. iv, p. 364.
[124] *Ibid.*, vol. iii, p. 339.
[125] Nightingale: p. 155.
[126] *Ibid.*, p. 184.
[127] Bradburn: *Meth. Set Forth*, p. 38.

of people where one might indulge in an intimate and personal conversation about his sins. One of the rules of the bands was, that each should speak "freely and plainly of the true state of our souls."[128] Each band was governed by a simple set of rules and in 1744, *Directions given to the Band Societies* were published.[129] There were at least twenty of these bands in London in 1745, and their average attendance was five or six and never over ten. No money was connected with these bands.[130] The purpose of having these bands consist all of women, or all of men, was to promote this perfect freedom of the members "to confess their faults to one another and pray for one another that they may be healed."[131] The purpose in other words, was to intensify that same type of work that was being done in the class. It was a form of intensive specialization. Because of this Wesley tried to give the bands that close attention which he bestowed upon the classes. "I fix an hour every day for speaking with each of the bands, that no disorderly walker might remain among them."[132] He saw to it that the *Rules of the Bands* were read over and kept.[133] The Church opposed these bands; because such intimate talks of religious matters it thought undesirable. The Methodists were thought to indulge in auricular confession within these bands.[134] So they did; but of a different type from that of the Church of Rome. The Roman Catholic confessed to the priest alone; the Methodist confessed to several of his fellow-laymen. Thus in the classes and bands we see two highly organized and specialized institutions to instruct in, and win loyalty to, the Methodist practices.

It was this tendency to concentrate in organization that brought in the steward to the Methodist societies. Wesley was burdened with much detail about financial matters. "A proposal was made for devolving all temporal business, books and all, entirely upon the stewards. . . . Oh, when shall it once be!"[135]

---

[128] *Works*, vol. v, p. 183.
[129] *Ibid.*, vol. v, p. 193ff.
[130] *Jour.*, vol. iii, p. 207.
[131] *Ibid.*, vol. ii, p. 174.
[132] *Ibid.*, vol. ii, p. 440.
[133] *Ibid.*, vol. iv, p. 186.
[134] Nightingale: p. 194.
[135] *Jour.*, vol. iv, p. 52.

The stewards, for this reason, were given complete charge of all temporal matters. As early as 1747 directions were given them in writing, for the governing of the London Society. If the stewards disobeyed these rules after three times, they would be put out of their stewardship.[136] Wesley laid down eleven rules governing the stewards of the Foundry at London. Each steward was to be present at the Foundry every Tuesday and Thursday morning to transact the temporal affairs of the society. The meetings were to be regular and orderly, and they were to consider the needs of the poor. They were always to treat the poor kindly; even though they were unable to grant them assistance.[137] Whosoever broke this rule ceased to be a steward. It was the duty of the stewards to keep an exact account of all expenses and expenditures, and their records show how faithful they were, even with the numerous small items which they dealt with.[138] They also had charge of an account from which they were to loan money to the needy. This was done on a somewhat extensive scale.[139]

Besides meeting the stewards in their work in connection with the local societies, Wesley also used to meet them in a body four times a year at what was called the "quarterly meeting." This quarterly meeting enabled Wesley to come into contact with many stewards especially those from the country. "Stewards from the country were present," he wrote.[140] And in another instance he noted, "Stewards met from the societies in the country." [141] And again we read, "We had a quarterly meeting, at which were present all the stewards from our Cornish societies." [142] From this it would appear that Wesley laid great stress upon the fact that stewards from the country places came out. This gave him an increased opportunity for strengthening Methodism in those remote places.

The leaders also came to this quarterly meeting and each

---

[136] *Works*, vol. vii, p. 486ff.
[137] *Jour.*, vol. iii, p. 300ff.
[138] W. H. S. *Proceedings*, vol. iii, p. 99ff.
[139] *Ibid.*, vol. iii, p. 197.
[140] *Jour.*, vol. iv, p. 394, and note i.
[141] *Ibid.*, vol. iv, p. 467.
[142] *Ibid.*, vol. iii, p. 491.

one brought with him his class paper showing what money he had actually received and turned over to the stewards. Bills were presented for payment. Preaching and worship took place.[143] But the quarterly meeting was held primarily to attend to the financial needs of the work.[144] It could not have been welcome to the stewards, for Wesley said of one such meeting: "This is frequently a dull and heavy meeting; but it was so lively a one to-day that we hardly knew how to part." [145] Not only the leaders but also the stewards rendered accounts at the quarterly meeting. These accounts were to show the progress or retrogression the societies had made.[146]

As the quarterly meeting tended to become a permanent institution within Methodism, it concerned itself with the work of one, and more and more, of but one circuit.[147] So it is that we read that the circuit of Yarm showed an increase of the poor; but the rich did not seem to care about religion.[148] Because the poor entered the societies and the rich remained without, it was always with difficulty that the quarterly meeting handled the item of money. A quarterly meeting of London reported that the income of its circuit was still less than expenses.[149] As late as February 29, 1790, Wesley recorded: "We had our general quarterly meeting, whereby it appears that the society received and expended about £3,000 a year; but our expense still exceeded our income." [150] Thus the quarterly meeting served to unite the stewards together in a greater sympathy for their common task, and to "diligently inquire both into the temporal and the spiritual state of each society." [151]

SECTION IV. THE METHODIST PRESS

Far more powerful in developing Methodist ideas and spirit, than any of the before-mentioned institutions, was the Methodist

---
[143] W. H. S. *Proceedings,* vol. vii, p. 80ff.
[144] *Jour.,* vol. vi, p. 305.
[145] *Ibid.,* vol. vi, p. 38.
[146] *Ibid.,* vol. v, p. 147.
[147] *Ibid.,* vol. v, p. 148.
[148] *Ibid.,* vol. v, p. 174.
[149] *Ibid.,* vol. v, p. 522.
[150] *Ibid.,* vol. viii, p. 40.
[151] W. H. S. *Proceedings,* vol. vii, p. 80.

118 THE SEPARATION OF THE METHODISTS

press. Wesley himself was a great lover and reader of books.[152] While travelling, he read the classics and the standard works of his day. His *Journals* tell of his opinion of what he read: Blackwell's *Sacred Classics Illustrated and Defended* he liked; a long book review was the result of his reading Dr. Parson's *Remains of Japheth.*[153] While he was going through Scotland, in one week he read *The History of Scotland* by Stuart.[154] He thought that Dr. Hunter's *Lectures* were too florid to be real good.[155] And as for a *Description of China and Chinese Tartary* he said, "Du Halde's word I will not take for a straw", for Du Halde was a Jesuit.[156] When Wesley considered reading to be so important for himself, it was most natural that he should esteem books and reading matter equally vital for his followers. In fact, this was his attitude, and he worked most diligently to meet the need.

While he was travelling from place to place, it was his custom to read many things for his *Christian Library.*[157] This library contained 233 volumes which Wesley felt his followers ought to read, not of original works, or even works that were rewritten; but rather, it was a plan of correcting the works of others, and publishing them. Wesley crossed out what he did not like in a given book, and this book was then printed with these omissions which Wesley had indicated.[158] This library was begun in 1749. Wesley also had good writers among his followers to support him in teaching his people the spirit and principles of Methodism, and in defending it before the world. John Fletcher, Joseph Benson, and Adam Clarke—no mean writers—contributed to the support of the Methodist press.[159]

The hymnals of early Methodism were an important product of the Methodist press. *The Hymns for the Nativity of our Lord,* wherein such hymns as, "Come thou long expected

---

[152] *Jour.,* vol. vii, p. 258.
[153] *Ibid.,* vol. vi, p. 333.
[154] *Ibid.,* vol. vii, p. 139.
[155] *Ibid.,* vol. vii, p. 232.
[156] *Ibid.,* vol. vii, p. 241.
[157] *Ibid.,* vol. vi, p. 325.
[158] Tyerman: vol. ii, p. 65ff.
[159] *Jour.,* vol. vi, p. 94.

FROM THE CHURCH OF ENGLAND 119

Saviour" appeared.[160] In 1756 a hymnal of twenty-four pages was published. To be sure, none of the great hymns of the Church appear in this early work; but when one remembers the fantastic hymns which the Moravians were producing at that time, this hymnal stands well by comparison. Between the years 1737 and 1767, John and Charles Wesley published not less than twenty-one different hymnals between them. Their first volume contained nine hymns; but their hymnal of 1789 contained 525 hymns.[161]

Liturgy was not forgotten. Wesley loved it and ever sought to have his services dignified through its use. "I believe there is no liturgy in the world, either in ancient or modern language, which breathes more of a solid, scriptural, rational piety, than the Common Prayer of the Church of England."[162] But in spite of this opinion, Wesley proceeded to publish a liturgy for his followers both in America and England, which differed from the Established Church and shortened most of its services.[163] This *Book of Prayer* contained: prayers for each day in the week, morning and evening; questions for personal interrogation; a collection of prayers for families, for morning and evening; prayers for children, which were quite theological and long; prayers for relatives; and grace to offer before and after meals. It was quite complete, and the Methodist who used it freely, would not be likely to resort to the Book of Common Prayer.[164]

The products of the press aided in the fixation of doctrine as well as the devotion in worship. Wesley published among other things his *Notes on the New Testament*. The ideas contained in these notes were not unique to Wesley. He laid no claim to originality, but frankly said that he borrowed from such celebrated men as: John Albert Bengel, professor in the theological seminary at Denkendorf, and a well known editor of a critical edition of the New Testament; Dr. John Heylin, a well known mystic who became prebendary of Westminster and a

---

[160] *Vide*, p. 14.
[161] W. H. S. *Proceedings*, vol. i, pp. 118-119.
[162] *Sunday Service of the Methodists*, p. 2.
[163] T. Jackson: *Life of C. Wesley*, p. 719.
[164] *Collection of Form of Prayer, passim.*

chaplain in ordinary to George III; Dr. John Guyse, an independent minister then known for his vigorous attacks upon Arianism; and Dr. Philip Doddridge, a nonconformist divine who wrote much in prose and many good hymns—these were some of the helpers of Wesley. In these notes, the cardinal beliefs of Methodism were put forth; and because of this, they became the standard creed of the Methodist meeting houses. In this way, one result of the press was to voice and also to solidify Methodist belief into a rigid mould. Each preacher was obliged to promise loyalty to the doctrines expressed in Wesley's *Notes* ere he could be permitted to preach.[165]

The great attempt to acquaint the people of England with the tenets of Methodism was the publishing of the *Arminian Magazine*. Wesley issued a prospectus for this undertaking, November 24, 1777. The magazine itself was to appear January 1, 1778. The purpose of it was to foster Methodism.[166] It would contain "no views, no politics, no personal invectives" but would be devoted to the uses of theology and vital religion.[167] Wesley superintended the editing and circulating of it. He instructed Joseph Taylor, the printer, to send copies of this magazine by sea to Bristol or London and if any copies were damaged en route, they could be sold for half price.[168] Concerning his toils as editor he said, "I looked over all the manuscripts which I had collected for the *Magazine,* destroyed what I did not think worth publishing, and corrected the rest." [169] One of the trials of Wesley's life was to keep this magazine free from errors. "This week I endeavored to point out all the errata in the eight volumes of the *Arminian Magazine.* This must be done by me; otherwise several pages therein will be unintelligible." [170] And when Wesley could stand the tribulation of a poor printer no longer, Thomas Olivers was dropped; because he made too many errors in his work, and because he inserted many pieces

---

[165] W. H. S. *Proceedings,* vol. ix, p. 97.
[166] *Jour.,* vol. vi, p. 168, note ii.
[167] Tyerman: vol. iii, p. 281ff.
[168] Eayrs: p. 210.
[169] *Jour.,* vol. vii, p. 337.
[170] *Ibid.,* vol. vii, p. 133.

into the magazine without Wesley's consent.[171] Wesley clearly saw the value of the *Arminian Magazine*.

The organization of the press was further completed by the appointing of certain men to act as "book stewards". As early as 1753, T. Butts and W. Briggs, both Methodist preachers, were appointed in this capacity. They strove to be business like; they demanded that an exact account be kept with each church; they required that payments for all stock be made at least every quarter; and they objected strenuously to the habit of the local stewards of taking money belonging to the book stewards and using it for other purposes. These men had the powers of an attorney to collect money for the books they had sold.[172] Unfortunately, all of the book stewards did not have equal ability or inclination. John Atlay, a book steward for fifteen years, made a report, September 20, 1788, and told Wesley that the value of the stock in the book room was £13,751, and not less. But Wesley complained after that it was less.[173] Indeed, he found that Atlay had overvalued his stock to the extent of £9,000 and that he was in a bad financial position. Selling books, hitherto, had not been very profitable from a financial point of view.[174]

After his trouble with John Atlay, Wesley appointed a committee to audit his accounts and business at the book room. He wished it to be better managed in the future. Wesley died, and George Whitefield in behalf of the Conference took charge of the book room until 1804. At that time, a committee of fifteen members of Conference were responsible for Methodist publications; but it could not serve in this capacity for more than six successive years.[175] Conference also took the pains to aid the book business by ruling in 1782, for a second time, that preachers should not publish anything without the consent of John Wesley, or at least his corrections, and that all funds coming from such publications should go into the common fund. This was done to

---

[171] *Ibid.*, vol. vii, p. 525ff.
[172] Tyerman: vol. ii, p. 176ff.
[173] W. H. S. *Proceedings*, vol. i, p. 90ff.
[174] *Works*, vol. vii, p. 332.
[175] Warren: vol. i, pp. 378-379.

prevent manuscripts with ideas distintegrating to the spirit of Methodism, and injurious to Methodism before the public, from being printed.[176] Later at the Conference of 1796, this was changed. To stop outside publishing, the author was to receive 100 copies of every 1,000 of his production that was sold; and if his articles were published in the *Arminian Magazine,* he was to be paid.[177] At last the press was upon a workable basis, and when such men as Adam Clarke, Samuel Bradburn, and Henry Moore, all well known Methodist historians, labored in its behalf, its success was quite assured.[178]

Wesley did all that he could to establish the press as an institution of Methodism, and to spread its publications abroad. He urged all of his people to adopt the habit of reading. "The societies are not half supplied with books; not even with *Jane Cooper's Letters,* or the two or three sermons which I printed last year."[179] Wesley firmly believed that loyal Methodists should buy Methodist publications.

In this way was the Methodist press developed. Of its value, Jackson, who wrote Methodist works after Wesley's death, said: "One of the most important and successful means adopted by the two Wesleys for promoting the interests of religion, was the publication, in a cheap and popular form, of a large number of interesting and instructive books."[180] The Methodist press aided immeasurably in binding the Methodists more firmly together in harmony of spirit. It freed them from dependence upon unsympathetic or unfriendly publications for their reading. It educated them to a greater loyalty to all Methodist institutions including itself. It worked with other organizations in promoting the doctrines and beliefs, the spirit and practices, of the Methodists. Around it centered a feeling of unity for Methodist principles. So long as the Methodists had this vigorous press, just so long was the opportunity for further unity with the Established Church impossible; for the Methodist press, as

---
[176] *Minutes.* vol. i, p. 153.
[177] *Ibid.,* vol. i, p. 345.
[178] *Ibid.,* vol. i, p. 276.
[179] *Letters, Works,* vol. vii, p. 7.
[180] *Centenary of Wesleyan Methodism,* p. 84.

an organization to further Methodism, constantly advocated Methodist unity and independence. To it in a large part, Methodism owed its very life.

Section V. Summary

We have seen the extent to which the Methodists went in their organization. They grouped themselves into societies that they might find the necessary sympathy to fortify one another to do what Methodists ought. Then the preachers of these societies met in their Conferences at least once a year to determine the general policies, and to fortify each other to preach what Methodists ought to preach. And after the societies were established, they were further divided into classes, that individual training in the practices and purposes of Methodism might take place. Later these classes were further subdivided in order to more intensively and individually carry on the work which the classes had undertaken to do. That financial support might not be neglected, certain ones were delegated as stewards to attend to this matter, and to nothing else. Stewards were required to attend the quarterly meetings for their edification and to gain wisdom and zeal in the conduct of financial matters.

Furthermore, all of this efficient detailed activity was kept under the direct supervision and control of Wesley and his assistants and preachers as they met in the Annual Conference. The Conference looked into the least detail. All things were done by rule, and in a legal, orderly fashion. This gave to it added strength as a centralizing power. It prevented the energies of Methodists from becoming scattered and consequently ineffective.

All of this was done to advance Methodist doctrines and Methodist practices. It was an evolution of an organization arising from a deep seated desire to save England. No one part of this organization was consciously planned a long time in advance, but grew out of the needs of the day. The important fact is: that after the Methodists had adopted every plan and method to spread their doctrines and their practices, they found themselves in possession of a strong, developed, and useful organization, which good sense would not allow them to discard lightly, and to keep which, added to their sense of unity, while it took away their feeling of need and dependence upon the Established Church.

Whatever might have been the avowals and desires of the Methodists, that their various organizations should force and teach loyalty to the Church, the very existence of these organizations worked in quite the opposite direction. The Methodists could not have an organization of their own, and have unity with the Established Church furthered at one and the same time. This was sociologically impossible.

CHAPTER VI

DEVELOPMENT OF METHODIST SOLIDARITY

SECTION I. WESLEY'S OPPOSITION TO THE UNIFICATION OF
METHODISM

MENTAL and practical differences such as peculiarities or standards of conduct are socializing forces, and to this the Methodists were no exception. There were practical differences between Churchmen and Methodists from the very beginning of the movement. As we have seen, the Methodists differed from the Church in the emphasis they placed upon doctrines such as the New Birth, and Christian Perfection. Then too, their preaching in the fields; their establishment of the itineracy; their use of lay preachers; their ordinations: all of these practices were considered by the Churchmen unnecessary and unjustifiable innovations. And finally, the various phases of Methodist organization such as the Conferences, classes, and quarterly meetings constituted a real difference.

The continuance of these practical differences had its effect upon the social grouping of the Methodists, for endlessly varied modes of love and hate tend ever to reconstruct and dominate social grouping.[1] The Methodists were fully aware of how much

---

[1] Giddings: *Readings in Descriptive and Historical Sociology*, p. 275.

they and the group to which they belonged differed from the Church, and this consciousness came to its own in their many pronounced expressions of opinion concerning the life about them, for nearly all Methodists were dissatisfied with the state of the Church and vital religion.[2] And the very opposition they received, stiffened their convictions so that this consciousness, which was at first somewhat vague, developed into a more or less definite emotion of mutual sympathy.

This type of sympathy among them was nothing abstract or unreal. "It is a power as real as that consciousness of disciplined strength which fights victorious battles, or as that consciousness of weakness and demoralization which hastens inglorious retreat."[3] It made the Methodists wish to organize more intensively to attain their common ends and to promote those beliefs and acivities which they felt England badly needed. No uniformity either of time or place characterized the steps they took; but before Wesley's death a vague consciousness had clarified itself into a distinct desire for greater combination to achieve Methodist purposes.

Yet Wesley, who in other respects was such a keen observer of the life about him, seemed not to understand the direction which the Methodist movement was surely taking; neither did he seem acquainted with this desire for greater unity and independence among the Methodists that so clearly marked the conduct of his followers. That the Methodists were becoming a distinct social entity, he repeatedly professed not to believe. Nor did he in the least desire the Methodists to be formed into a body separate from the Church, and his personal actions neither sanctioned nor countenanced the taking of any steps connected with his organization that would result in separation. He was frankly opposed to leaving the Church.

Wesley professed great loyalty to the Church of England. "I live and die a member of the Church of England."[4] This

---

[2] *Vide*, chap. i.
[3] Giddings: *Op. cit.*, p. 326.
[4] Lecky: *Hist. of Eng. in 18th Century*, vol. ii, p. 688.

loyalty did not hinder him from advocating for his followers a higher type of piety than was commonly practiced by the members of the Church.[10] In a phrase that must have been irritating to the clergy he said: "It is very possible to be united to Christ and to the Church of England at the same time. . . . we do not need to separate from the Church in order to preserve allegiance to Christ; but may be firm members thereof, and yet 'have a conscience void of offense toward God and man.'"[11]

To be sure, he did write to his brother saying, "I do not at all think (to tell you the truth) that the work will ever be destroyed, Church or no Church."[12] Yet this attitude is outdone when it is remembered that he was quite particular to bury his mother according to the rites of the Church of England.[13] In 1758, a tract entitled, *Reasons Against a Separation from the Church of England* was published. Here, Wesley gave twelve reasons why the Methodists should remain within the Church. So heartily was Charles Wesley—the High Churchman—in accord with this statement that he seconded it with his signature.[14]

Wesley showed that he assumed the Methodists to be members of the Church, when in an address to the king on March 5, 1744, he asserted: "that we are a part (however mean) of that Protestant Church established in these kingdoms."[15] He also approved Middleton's *Essay on Church Government;* because it neither exalted nor depressed the regal power; but kept the middle way.[16] All of this sounded much like good churchmanship, and when as late as 1782 he was asked, "Is it your wish that the people called Methodists should be, or become, a body separate from the Church?"—he answered as upon former occasions, "No."[17] Mr. W. E. H. Lecky, authority on Irish affairs and the writer of those famous volumes, *England in the Eighteenth Century*, was correct when he said, "Nothing can

---
[10] *Jour.*, vol. ii, p. 86.
[11] *Letter to Mr. Toogood, Works*, vol. vi, p. 234.
[12] Tyerman: vol. ii, p. 416.
[13] *Jour.*, vol. iii, p. 30, note ii.
[14] *Works*, vol. vii, p. 293ff.
[15] *Jour.*, vol. iii, p. 123.
[16] *Ibid.*, vol. iii, p. 42.
[17] Moore: vol. ii, p. 238.

be more unjust than to attribute to him the ambition of a schismatic, or the subversive instincts of a revolutionist."[18]

Since Wesley, as leader, felt thus loyal to the Church, one is not surprised to find that he and others worked for the unity of the Methodists with it. Between Wesley and Mr. Walker, of Truro, there was much correspondence on this head. Walker said that Wesley intended to be a schismatic; but Wesley answered Walker to the contrary by saying, "Tell me what, and I will do it without delay, however contrary it may be to my ease or natural inclination."[19] Here Wesley said he would do anything save give up his flock in order that he might not be schismatic. At another time he wrote to Walker saying that the clergy were all too worldly and inefficient to meet the needs of the day; and that while such a condition lasted, the Methodists could not more heartily unite with the Church.[20] Mr. Walker also came forth with the suggestion that Methodist lay preachers be ordained in the Church; not as preachers, but as inspectors and readers. These he would have stationed in certain societies. Wesley objected that the lay preachers had not enough talent to remain in one place for a long period of time—fixed lay preachers became dead and inefficient.[21] Walker continued this matter and urged Wesley to do away with his lay preachers, saying that there could be no unity while lay preachers were used by the Methodists. To this persuasion Wesley replied, "I am still desirous of knowing in what particular manner you think the present work of God could be carried on without assistance of lay preachers."[22] He would not give up his lay preachers to gain unity.

Wesley also wrote a circular letter to the clergy, asking them to meet with him that they might discuss the basis upon which unity might take place. No attention was paid to this suggestion.[23] The clergy knew Wesley's proneness to ask advice and not take it too well.

---

[18] Lecky: *Op. cit.*, vol. ii, p. 687.
[19] Moore: vol. ii, p. 166.
[20] *Ibid.*, pp. 172-174.
[21] *Works*, vol. vii, p. 276ff.
[22] *Ibid.*, vol. vii, p. 281.
[23] Moore: vol. ii, pp. 167-169.

FROM THE CHURCH OF ENGLAND

Some effort, however, was made on the part of the clergy to gain unity with the Methodists. One Churchman said that the Methodists had scant appreciation for the "necessity and indispensable duty of Church unity." This lack of appreciation was the cause of dissent.[24] Such scolding did not appeal to the Methodists. Zachary Grey urged Methodist laymen to stay within the Church, and pointed out the advantage of having a fixed liturgy about which the Methodists could rally their loyalty. But then, as now, there was no compromise. If the Methodists would enter the Established Church, they must adjust themselves to it. It would not adjust itself to them.[25]

The Mehodist writers, David Simpson and Samuel Bradburn, discussed this question of unity quite adequately. Simpson said that Methodist ministers should be held as helpers, coadjutors, and not as enemies of the Church. There could be no thought of unity until this was done.[26] Bradburn was more thoroughgoing; he advocated: that traveling preachers of long standing should be ordained in the Established Church; that no preachers be ordained by the bishops unless recommended by Conference; that the ordained Methodist preachers be permitted to bury, baptize, and administer the Lord's Supper, provided they receive no pay therefor; that the Church service only be used in meeting houses in Church hours; that the plan of itineracy, circuits, districts, Conferences, remain untouched; that the bishops of the Established Church be present at the Conference when the preachers and probationers have their characters examined, and that these bishops have the authority to bring charges against Methodist preachers. Bradburn would also have Methodist meeting houses registered and have them pay a yearly sum to the bishops. "Such are the rough outlines of a scheme, that if adopted, might bring half a million people into the strictest union with the Church. And if something of this kind be not done, will not those be to blame who oppose it—I am not one of these."[27] Thus earnest attempts were for Church unity.

---
[24] *The Question*, p. 4.
[25] Grey: *Serious Address to Lay Methodists*, p. 4ff.
[26] *Happiness of Dying in the Lord*, passim.
[27] Bradburn: *The Question*, pp. 20-21.

SECTION II. BISHOPS OF THE ESTABLISHED CHURCH AND METHODISM

The attitude of the bishops of the Established Church alone would have made null and void any progress toward unity between the Churchmen and the Methodists.

It must not be supposed that there was no exception to this unfriendliness of the bishops. In Ireland, Wesley supported Archbishop Cobbe, when that prelate urged the formation of a society for the distribution of books among the poor.[28] With the Bishop of Londonderry Wesley had a real friendship.[29] This bishop manifested his friendliness toward Wesley in a letter saying, "It would have given me very sincere pleasure to have seen you during your stay in Dublin. . . . Indeed, I did not expect your stay would have been so short."[30] Wesley in turn showed his admiration for the bishop by noting: "The bishop preached a judicious, useful sermon on the blasphemy of the Holy Ghost. He is both a good writer and a good speaker; and he celebrated the Lord's Supper with admirable solemnity."[31]

The relationships between the Bishop of Londonderry and the Methodists were not characteristic of the times. Many bishops disliked the Methodists; William Warburton, Bishop of Gloucester, was extremely violent in his abuse of the Wesleys, and attacked them in a most personal manner.[32] Dr. Coke remodeled his parish of Petherton somewhat after the fashion of a circuit. On Sundays, after the second lesson, he would read a paper of his appointments for the ensuing week, with the place and time of his service.[33] Because of this Coke was dismissed from his curacy by the bishop, and he resolved to cast his lot with the Methodists. Wesley thought this dismissal the deed of a bigot.[34] Overton said: "It is fair to add that this dismissal from his curacy can hardly be regarded as an act of

---

[28] *Jour.*, vol. iv, p. 259.
[29] *Ibid.*, vol. v, p. 511.
[30] Whitehead: vol. ii, p. 289.
[31] *Jour.*, vol. vi, p. 65.
[32] Fitchett: p. 344.
[33] Tyerman: vol. iii, p. 214.
[34] *Jour.*, vol. vi, p. 169.

tyranny."³⁵ But the Methodists of that time actually felt just the contrary.

The motives which prompted the bishops to go against the Methodists were sometimes very sincere and sensible. In a most moderate manner, Bishop Gibson wrote: "God forbid that in this profane and degenerate age, everything that has the appearance of piety and devotion should not be considered in the most favorable light that it is capable of. But at the same time it is surely very proper that men should be called upon for some *reasonable* evidences of a divine commission from God, a. when they use the language of those who have a commission from God, b. when they profess to think and act under divine inspiration, c. when they claim the effects of preaching as a work of divine power, d. when they boast of the result of their preaching as the work of the Holy Ghost, e. when they claim the spirit of prophecy, f. when they speak of themselves in the language and under the character of apostles of Christ, g. when they claim to propagate a new gospel." The bishop analyzed the *Journals* of Whitefield and brought these objections to them in this orderly manner.³⁶ Gibson did not like this enthusiasm; he considered that "it is one thing to pray *for* the Holy Spirit, and another to pray *by* the Holy Spirit." Few people had any ability to pray in public; hence the bishop took a stand against it.³⁷ This position taken by Gibson had much influence. His *Pastoral Letter of 1739* was widely read and went through several editions; above all, it tried to deal with facts.³⁸ Wesley replied to Gibson and argued to the point, that the bishop was not careful to distinguish the Methodists from the Moravians; and that both were quite distinct groups.³⁹ But the bishop could not be persuaded, and he continued his opposition to Methodist teachers on the ground that they were boastful and vainglorious; and they thought themselves to be doing some especially great work. Gibson brought out good evidence to prove this point, for the Methodists very

---
³⁵ *Life of Wesley*, p. 154.
³⁶ *Pastoral Letter, 1739*, p. 16ff.
³⁷ *Ibid.*, p. 15.
³⁸ *Vide* Bibliography.
³⁹ *Works*, vol. v, p. 341.

bluntly said theirs was the task of reforming the Church. Most naturally the bishops could not tolerate the imputation of such corruption to their Church.[40] Nevertheless, the Bishop of London was not clear cut in his stand. He could find fault, and that ably; but he could not suggest a remedy. He said that true Christianity lay between the excesses of the enthusiasts and the lukewarmness of irreligion.[41] Gibson was correct in this. And when Fitchett says of him: "He, like many of his clergy, held the curious theory that the Divine Spirit acted everywhere in general, but nowhere in particular; while the deluded Methodists taught the incredible doctrine that the Holy Spirit worked in individual souls," it would seem that Fitchett did not do Gibson justice for his well thought out position.[42]

All the bishops, however, did not show the restraint of Gibson in their objections to the enthusiasm of the Methodists. John Green, Bishop of Lincoln, could not see any outward signs that the Methodists could meet their claims.[43] Butler, the author of the *Analogy* and Bishop of Bristol, denounced Whitefield and Wesley for their actions. "I hear, too, that many persons fall into fits in your societies and that you pray over them." The bishop objected to this way of doing things and advised Wesley to quit preaching here and yonder; to settle down; and to cease to break the law of the Church. Wesley told the bishop point blank, that he would work wherever he could do the most good.[44] Lavington, of course, had to be violent: "It is but too notorious, that the same enthusiasm under the same management, hath driven numbers of these unhappy creatures into direct madness and distraction, either of a moping, or raving kind."[45] Lavington drew up much proof for this statement; just and fair proof —which was just contrary to his usual method of attack.

The bishops of the Church saw the moral conditions of their time, and were concerned for it. Archbishop Secker, in 1738, openly said: "An open and professed disregard for reli-

[40] *Observations Upon Conduct of Meth.*, p. 22.
[41] *Pastoral Letter*, p. 4.
[42] Fitchett: p. 340.
[43] *Principles and Practices of Methodists*, p. 24ff.
[44] Whitehead: vol. ii, pp. 120-121.
[45] *Enthusiasm, etc.*, p. 177.

gion is become, through a variety of unhappy causes, the distinguishing character of the present age." He figured crime and bad living to be on the increase. The clergy were not influential; they were laughed at; they led base lives. He urged people everywhere to take life seriously.[46] Gibson, too, in his thoroughgoing manner went into the situation confronting the Church in detail. He warned the people against lukewarmness in religion. He railed against formal Church attendance, and pleaded that the people should learn to delight in real devotion and private prayer. Sincere dislike of gross evil in self and in others was the test of true religion which he set up. People were playing at religion. "And there is danger of their being led to think too favorably of their condition, in an age which affords them so many examples of notorious and open wickedness, and a total neglect of the public worship of God."[47] Truly Gibson saw clearly.

In the light of the above conviction, Gibson scored the people. Personal attendance at Church, without attention and devotion, was not an act of religion. Men should regard their stations in life as God's appointments and should serve them as such. The Word of God and not the opinions of the world should be the measure of man's duty. Strict observance of one branch of duty was no excuse for the neglect of another part. Thus Gibson spoke vigorously for a clean Church and national life.[48] "It must always be remembered, in the first place, that we are Christian preachers, and not barely preachers of morality.[49]

Bishop Butler in his famous *Analogy* expresses his view by saying, "It is come, I know not how, to be taken for granted, by many persons, that Christianity is not so much a subject for inquiry; but that it is, now at length, discovered to be fictitious. And accordingly they treat it, as if, in the present age, this were an agreed point among all people of discernment; and nothing

---

[46] *Eight Charges,* ed. 4, 1790—quoted in Jackson: *Cent. of Wes. Meth.,* pp. 18-19.
[47] *Pastoral Letter,* p. 5.
[48] *Ibid.,* pp. 6-11.
[49] *Ibid.,* p. 25.

remained but to set it up as a principle of mirth and ridicule, for its having so long interrupted the mirth and pleasure of the world."[50] Thus the bishops were very much concerned with the state of affairs in their day, and felt that every effort should be put forth within the Church to remove the crying evils which they recognized as clearly as anyone else.

With this in mind, it can be seen how the bishops viewed the Methodist movement. They felt that it prevented the Church from facing the evils of the day with a solid front. Butler told Wesley, "If you desire to be extensively useful, do not spend your time and strength contending for or against such things as are of a disputable nature; but in testifying against open, notorious vice, and in promoting real, essential holiness."[51] This was splendid advice to anybody, and this was just what Wesley was doing. But the bishops undoubtedly felt that the Methodists caused strife and contention within the Church and thereby weakened its power to combat evil.

The bishops felt that Methodist doctrine was disturbing to the Church. Wesley was accused of holding the doctrine of "sinless perfection." He denied to the Bishop of London that he held this doctrine or that he even knew what it meant.[52] Lavington cited John Wesley as telling a woman that she was in hell if she had not the assurance of salvation. Wesley investigated this accusation and in *A second letter to the author of enthusiasm of the Methodists and Papists compared,* he showed Lavington had told an untruth.[53] Lavington continued his attack and said that scepticism, infidelity, doubts, and denials of the truth of revelation, and sometimes even atheism itself resulted from the Methodists.[54]

Not only Methodist doctrine, but also Methodist morality disturbed the Church. Gibson intimated that the Methodists were not careful for their conduct.[55] Bishop Horne as vice-chancellor, before the University of Oxford called the Meth-

---
[50] *Butler's Analogy,* Advertisement, p. b. 2.
[51] Southey: vol. ii, p. 202.
[52] *Works,* vol. v, p. 347.
[53] *Ibid.,* vol. v, p. 373ff.
[54] *Enthusiasm, etc.,* p. 125.
[55] Jackson: *Cent. of Meth.,* p. 17.

odists "the new lights of the tabernacle and the Foundry," and accused them of teaching a bad faith and a lax morality.[56]

The organization of the Methodists was also thought to weaken the Church. Gibson gives the list—bands and societies; superintendents; exhorters; quarterly meetings; moderators; visitations—these are all unwarranted in the law and are therefore illegal.[57] Archbishop Robinson objected to lay preaching.[58]

Thus on every hand, and for every conceivable reason, the Methodists found themselves opposed by the bishops. Some of these bishops showed sanity in their opposition, others showed none. For this reason the Methodists did not trouble themselves to obey the bishops in all things. Whitefield was said to show scant courtesy to the bishops.[59] But though the bishops were wrong in their judgments and slow in their actions, Churchmen felt that they were the constituted authorities of the Church and as such should be obeyed until "they should judge it proper to revoke or supersede themselves."[60] The Methodists were no worshipers of the episcopacy, especially when they thought these bishops to stand in their way for saving England.

Yet the Methodists would not admit that they broke any Church law in their unhappy relationships with the bishops. "Are you not guilty of canonical disobedience to your bishops?" Wesley was asked. "I think not. Show me wherein," was his answer.[61] Wesley did not, however, think himself subjected to the will of a bishop. "But did you not take oath to obey him?" Wesley's reply was emphatic, "No, nor any clergyman in the three kingdoms. This is a mere vulgar error."[62] Under this treatment Wesley evolved his idea of Church government. "As to my own judgment, I still believe 'the episcopal form of Church government to be Scriptural and apostolical,' I mean, well agreeing with the practice and the writings of the apostles. But that it is inscribed in Scripture, I do not see." This opinion,

---

[56] Fitchett: p. 343.
[57] *Conduct of Methodists*, p. 20ff.
[58] *Meth. Mag., 1822*, p. 783.
[59] Gibson: *Earnest Appeal*, p. 8.
[60] Downes: *Methodism Examined*, p. 100.
[61] *Letter to T. H., Works*, vol. vii, p. 402.
[62] *Jour.*, vol. vi, p. 152.

which Wesley formerly accepted, he now rejected. "Neither Christ nor the apostles prescribe any form of Church government," he concluded.[63] The trend of thought from Wesley's utterance to this day seems to bear this statement out.

Thus have we seen that the attitude of the bishops worked against unity. Whether they were justified in holding such views is not the question. The Methodists grew bitter and more bitter against the Church as a result of this treatment, and at last came to a frame of mind where they thought bishops not needful, but an evil. Yet the bishops took even one more step away from any possibility of unity. They confused the Methodists with Roman Catholics.

SECTION III. CONFUSION OF METHODISTS WITH CATHOLICS

Roman Catholicism was not at all popular in England. People had not forgotten the days of James II. Catholic intrigue was sufficiently active in England to keep the suspicions of the people keyed to the highest pitch. Bishop Porteus, of Chester, wrote to the people of his parish and warned them against the efforts of the Catholics to make headway in England. The Catholics, said he, tried to make converts by: a. attempting bribery, b. by intermarrying with members of the Established Church, and c. by the practice of Catholics of showing a preference for Catholic labor. Bishop Porteus even went into detailed instructions for the people, informing them how best they could prevent this Catholic propaganda from going ahead. a. Parents were to keep their personal influence over their children as long as possible, b. they were to send their children to Protestant schools, and c. they were to read nothing save Protestant publications.[64] "The true secret, in short, for checking the growth of popery, or any other corrupt religion, is, lenity and vigilance in conjunction."[65] This was the suspicious attitude which all England adopted toward any form of Roman Catholicism during the eighteenth century.

During the Stuart uprising in the north in 1745, Wesley

---
[63] *Works*, vol. vii, p. 284.
[64] Porteus: *Letter to the Clergy of Chester*, pp. 7-10.
[65] *Ibid.*, p. 22.

FROM THE CHURCH OF ENGLAND

came under suspicion of papacy, and therefore treason. While the whole countryside was in an uproar, Wesley knowing himself to be under suspicion, visited one named Adams, an ex-priest, twice during these weeks of peril.[66] There was little sense in Wesley's doing this. He was accused of being a papist, an advocate of the Pretender, of traveling through France and Spain in behalf of the house of Stuart.[67] The Methodists were said to be masked Jesuits.[68]

One result of this was that Bishop Lavington launched his great polemic upon the Methodists, *The Enthusiasm of the Methodists and the Papists Compared.* In this work Lavington compared the Methodists with old Catholic enthusiasts, such as Saint Francis, a "weak enthusiast"; Saint Dominic, "a contriver and manager of the blessed instrument of conversion"; or Loyola, a "visionary fanatic or scatter brain." All of these Catholics indulged in field preaching as did the Methodists.[69] Furthermore, the system of the itineracy was compared with the pilgrimages and crusades of the Catholics—both were mere tricks to win admirers.[70] Both Catholics and Methodists laid claims to divine direction, to the presence of God, to raptures and ecstasies; and these claims were all humbug. "When the blood and spirits run high, inflaming the brain and imagination, it is most properly enthusiasm; which is religion run mad."[71] The Methodists and Papists even used the Scriptures in the same spirit. "They cannot open the Bible, and thereby turn the Holy Scriptures into a lottery, but they are sure of a prize. . . . or some special direction. They cannot read or hear lessons, psalms, epistles, and gospels, but they have sagacity enough to find something peculiarly concerning themselves." Thus the Methodists are quite as egotistical as the Catholics who lived long before them.[72]

There can be no doubt that Lavington had a genuine fear

---

[66] *Jour.,* vol. iii, p. 209.
[67] *Ibid.,* vol. iii, p. 191.
[68] Scott: *Op. cit.,* p. iv.
[69] Lavington: *Op cit.,* p. 6ff.
[70] *Ibid.,* p. 17.
[71] *Ibid.,* p. 53.
[72] *Ibid.,* p. 71.

of enthusiasm. The Methodists did have some isolated traits similar to the Catholics. But how a man of Lavington's position and intelligence could ever fail to distinguish between the Methodists and the Catholics we cannot understand. How sincerely he believed his main argument is open to doubt. The Methodists usually have looked upon him as the great Nero of their day, and one cannot well blame them.

Wesley clearly realized that he was accused of papist opinions.[73] He did what he could to enlighten his enemies. He wrote many letters to *Lloyd's Weekly*, answering the charges of papacy made against him.[74] He was very clear in his statements. Once he called the rulers of the Catholic Church since the days of Cyprian, "a conspiracy of execrable wretches."[75] There was little leaning toward the papacy in such a statement. Later on, he wrote: "I insist upon it that no government, not Roman Catholic, ought to tolerate men of Roman Catholic persuasion ... who cannot give security to that government for their allegiance and peaceable behavior."[76] This was quite loyal, and also quite anti-Catholic. In 1780 he wrote a letter that was quite lengthy in dealing with this question of Catholicism: the supremacy of the pope; the granting of pardons; and the truthfulness of Roman Catholics. This letter was so strong that Tyerman called it "obnoxious."[77] After this one would be insane to confuse the Methodists with the Papists. They were quite unlike in either loyalty or spirit.

SECTION IV. OPPOSITION TO THE METHODISTS

Not only by the bishops but also by learned men, publishers, and others, the Methodists were attacked. Early in the movement, relationships with Oxford were not friendly. In 1768, six students were expelled because they were Methodists and attended conventicles.[78] Whitefield was very wroth over this. Such meetings as in reality plotted against the state were for-

---

[73] *Jour.*, vol. ii, p. 263.
[74] *Ibid.*, vol. iv, p. 418ff.
[75] *Ibid.*, vol. iv, p. 96.
[76] *Ibid.*, vol. vi., p. 267.
[77] Tyerman: vol. iii, p. 318ff.
[78] *Ibid.*, vol. iii, p. 33.

bidden; but these students were ejected for praying extempore and reading and singing hymns. This was all unjust—such was Whitefield's conclusion.[79] Sarcastically an anonymous writer noted: "What miracle was it my beloved, that out of so much hundreds of students as are at Oxford, only six should be found guilty of praying, reading, and expounding the Scriptures. This shows the faithfulness of their vigilant tutors in guarding them against such pernicious practices."[80] But the authorities were firm and these students stayed out.

Wesley himself fared little better. Inasmuch as he was a fellow of Lincoln College, it was necessary for him to preach once a year at Saint Mary's. Such sermons as Wesley preached at Saint Mary's he carefully wrote out; sometimes in Latin as well as in English. No one seemed to encourage him. He was told that it made little difference what he preached about, for no one would care anyhow.[81] Some of the college authorities even took Wesley to be a little crack-brained, and frankly told him so.[82] But Wesley was not the man to shed tears over such treatment; when this opposition and indifference confronted him, he prepared to preach so that those who opposed him should sit up and take notice.

August 24, 1744, was the last time he was asked to preach at Saint Mary's. He sought to persuade his hearers frankly to admit that they had never seen a Christian country upon this earth. He asked the self-complacent college authorities if they were full of the Holy Ghost. He indicted his hearers in asserting that righteousness and Christianity were not characteristic of the Fellows of the College, and concluded his sermon with the petition: "Lord, take us out of the mire that we sink not."[83] It was a ringing challenge to the religious deadness of Oxford, but was most ungratefully received. Dr. Kennicott recorded that "the assertion that Oxford was not a Christian city, and this country not a Christian nation, were the most offensive

---

[79] Whitefield: *Letter to Dr. Durell*, pp. 13-14.
[80] The Shaver: *Priestcraft Defended*, p. 10.
[81] *Jour.*, vol. ii, p. 478.
[82] *Ibid.*, vol. ii, p. 243.
[83] *Works*, vol. i, *Sermon iv*.

parts of the sermon, except when he accused the whole body ... of the sin of perjury."[84] Wesley irritated his hearers. It was no wonder that the Vice-Chancellor wished to see the manuscript and Wesley recorded, "I preached I suppose for the last time at Saint Mary's. Be it so. I am now clear of the blood of these men. I have fully delivered my own soul."[85]

This was the beginning of the end; yet it was not until June 1, 1751, that Wesley wrote to the Rector and Fellows of Lincoln: "Ego Johannes Wesley, Collegii Lincolniensis in Academia Oxoniensis Socius, quicquid mihi juris est in praedicta Societate, ejusdem Rectori et Sociis sponte ac libere resigno; illis universis et singulis perpetuam pacem ac omnimodam in Christo felicitatem exoptans." Thus he resigned his fellowship, and the last thread of connection with Oxford was broken.[86] Opposition in Oxford resulted in a break with Oxford.

The opposition of the Churchmen characteristic at Oxford was continued in other forms and places. Opposition developed into general persecution. At Wednesbury, a mob maltreated a certain Joshua Constable's wife and wrecked his house—all because he was a Methodist.[87] Charles Wesley reported that five engines were played upon the house where he resided, and bulldogs were urged on to his horses.[88] Time and again John Wesley suffered physical abuse and nearly lost his life. This violent physical persecution was not common after 1751-2.[89] Not all joined in this violence. The vicar of Saint Martin's Church flayed those who tore down houses with the text: "Ye know not what manner of spirit ye are of." He threatened to leave his parish if his people did not conduct themselves more lawfully.[90] This attitude, however, was the exception rather than the rule.

Other forms of persecution continued. Farces were given holding the Methodists up to ridicule. One such play, *Trick*

---

[84] *Meth. Mag., 1866*, p. 44.
[85] *Jour.*, vol. iii, p. 147.
[86] *Cf. Jour.*, June 1, 1751.
[87] *Jour.*, vol. iii, p. 117ff.
[88] Charles Wesley: *Journal*, vol. i, pp. 442-449.
[89] *Jour.*, vol. iv., pp. 3 and 18.
[90] *Ibid.*, vol. iv, p. 37.

Upon Trick, was given at Newcastle. It was not a success, because the beams supporting the theater gave way soon after the play had started.[91] Many foul and bitter attacks were made upon the Methodists even at the beginning of the movement. Wesley's and Whitefield's journals were raked over and attacked. It is not our purpose to bring in all the evidence for this persecution; because that is not the purpose of this work and has been done more adequately elsewhere.[92] Our purpose is simply to note that opposition was the historic fact. Wesley did not desire "that anyone who thinks us heretics or schismatics, and that thinks it his duty to preach or print against us, as such, should refrain therefrom, so long as he thinks it is his duty. Although in this case the break can never be healed."[93] Wesley saw where this opposition was leading.

Other opposition came because the Methodists would not declare themselves Dissenters. Either they must close their meeting houses, or else they must have them licensed as Dissenters.[94] The Methodists would do neither. Sermons were preached against them to the effect that they sailed under false colors, inasmuch as they did not come out as Dissenters.[95] The Methodists would not take advantage of the Act of Toleration, for so doing would make them *ipso facto* Dissenters. They proposed rather to be fined for holding conventicles before they would dissent.[96] Yet the Methodists stoutly maintained their antipathy to Dissent: "We are not Dissenters in the only way our law acknowledges, namely, those who renounce the service of the Church. We do not, dare not, separate from it. We are not seceders nor do we bear any resemblance to them. We set out upon quite opposite principles. . . . They (the seceders) begin everywhere with showing their hearers how fallen the Church and ministers are: we begin everywhere by showing how

---

[91] *Ibid.,* vol. iii, p. 110.
[92] I refer to Barr's *Early Methodists Under Persecution.* This is the latest and best account of this opposition and for fuller evidence should be consulted at length.
[93] *Jour.,* vol. iii, p. 168.
[94] Lecky: *Op. cit.,* vol. ii, p. 689.
[95] John Free: *Sermon, 1758.*
[96] Tyerman: vol. iii, p. 512ff.

our hearers are themselves. What they do in America, or what their ministers say on this subject, is nothing to us. We will keep in the good way."[97] The Methodists desired to stay in the Church.

So far, we have seen that the Methodists faced opposition in connection with their doctrine, their practices, their organization, and that the bishops opposed them and confused them with Roman Catholics. We have seen that Wesley and others professed a desire to remain in the Church and stay loyal to it; but that in spite of this, a separation from Oxford took place, and the opposition in the forms of mobs, riots, persecutions, continued unabated. According to sociological laws, there could be but one result from all this.

Opposition caused "concerted volition" to further develop.[98] A considerable majority of the Methodists had reacted similarly to the stimulus of this opposition and the resemblance among them resulting from this reaction is called "like-mindedness." Opposition resulted in making the Methodists more or less "like-minded."[99]

At first the Methodists were like-minded in their sympathies; but as the opposition continued they became impatient of criticism and less and less disposed to be conciliatory. Their like-mindedness was becoming "formal."[100] Still the opposition continued and this like-mindedness became "deliberate," that is, the Methodists were "characterized by critical thinking, and moderate, well-coordinated action."[101] Methodists had discussed their grievances, fought off their adversaries, faced their opponents; but in doing so they had developed from a scattered, unorganized number of people into a group who were alike in mind and purpose, and who were alike because they had thought and reasoned. There can be, sociologically, but one outcome from such a development; the Methodists would be obliged to cooperate. "If consciousness of kind exists, then cooperation is

---

[97] *Large Minutes, Works,* vol. v, p. 227.
[98] See above, p. 140.
[99] Giddings: *Op. cit.,* p. 332.
[100] *Ibid., Op. cit.,* p. 339.
[101] *Ibid.,* p. 344.

sure to follow."[102] This cooperation had much opportunity ahead of it. "The highest development of cooperation is seen in the formulation of certain great policies through deliberation upon the character, the composition, and the circumstances of the community, and in efforts, both public and voluntary, to carry them to realization."[103]

This is just what happened with the Methodists. They drew closer and closer together as a result of this opposition, and finally their sense of solidarity was so keen that they here and there began to cooperate to further their solidarity. When they reached this stage of action and of thinking, they did not feel the need of the Established Church. They could get along with it. Opposition had made them strong, and more or less of a unit. The fact to make clear is: That the Methodists had reached that point of sociological solidarity where they felt able to conduct the affairs of their group in a manner satisfactory to themselves and without outside intervention.

[102] *Ibid.*, p. 353.
[103] *Ibid.*, p. 395.

CHAPTER VII

THE ACTUAL SEPARATION AFTER THE DEATH OF WESLEY

It must not be assumed from the discussion of the previous chapter that the development of solidarity among the Methodists was evenly uniform in every separate society and at every stated epoch. This sense of solidarity varied in proportion to the amount of opposition which the Methodists of any given place had felt themselves to have experienced at the hands of the Established Church. Hence the situation was complex: some felt strongly the unity of the Methodists, and possessed also the resulting strong desire to get away from the Church; others felt this solidarity less, and had less desire, if any at all, to get away from the Church. With such different points of view, unity of action could come only after struggle.

SECTION I. PATERNAL GOVERNMENT

The first intimation that the Methodists were not uniformly alike in their thinking came from within their own ranks and against their own leader. The government of the Methodists had been quite paternal, for Wesley was an autocrat in the most correct sense of that word. He claimed the absolute right before the society of Bath to appoint exactly whom he wished to serve them, and did not exercise this right in the most diplomatic manner.[1] When this question arose again, Wesley said, "To me the preachers have engaged themselves to submit; to serve me as sons in the gospel. To me the people in general will submit; but they will not yet submit to any other." Wesley clearly pointed out that this submission was purely voluntary; nevertheless, he frankly admitted his power.[2]

It was undoubtedly Wesley's aim to keep this paternal form of government perpetual. In 1773 he wrote a long letter to John

---
[1] Tyerman: vol. iii, p. 305.
[2] *Ibid.*, vol. ii, p. 579.

Fletcher, urging him to head the Methodist movement when Wesley died. Fletcher being much younger than Wesley, it was to be expected that Wesley should die first. Wesley asserted that Fletcher was qualified to fill this position better than anyone else in the connection, but Fletcher was of a different mind and refused to accept this future position.[3]

Not all Methodists enjoyed this paternal government. Alexander M'Nab rebelled against it; whereupon, Wesley expelled him from the Methodist ministry. Wesley here intended to put down a real rebellion and maintain a central authority in Methodism; yet Tyerman deems it an injustice to M'Nab, for the way in which he was treated.[4] If there were murmurings against the Methodist system as it existed while Wesley was alive, when he died it was to be expected that these complaints would increase.

On Wesley's death, many issues which had been smouldering, broke into flame. The strong central figure was no longer there to place his weighty influence where it would most steady that good ship—Methodism.

SECTION II. THE EUCHARIST

The Church of England in its effort to meet the worldliness of the 18th century was urging its members to a more frequent communion. Archbishop Tillotson in *A Persuasive to Frequent Communion* represents this trend.[5] Wesley vigorously supported this view and continually preached upon the duty of constant communion, insisting that yearly communion was not enough. The duty of every Christian was to communicate as often as he could.[6] Wesley constantly administered the communion to his societies and kept up this habit to the end. "After reading prayers, preaching, and administering the communion at Bristol, I hastened away to Kingswood."[7] These services were well attended. At London between 1600 and 1700 persons

---

[3] *Letter, Works,* vol. vi, p. 688.
[4] Vol. iii, p. 309.
[5] *Qui vide.*
[6] *Sermon, Works,* vol. ii, p. 349ff.
[7] *Ibid.,* vol. vi, p. 129.

joined in the sacramental service and Wesley secured five ordained clergymen to help him.[8]

No objection was made to this administration on the part of Wesley. The "good old" dean of St. Patrick's Cathedral, in Ireland, Dr. Francis Corbett, desired him to come within the rails to assist him at the Lord's Supper[9] And after some of the heat of controversy had cooled a little, Wesley was "well pleased to partake of the Lord's Supper with my old opponent, Bishop Lavington." [10]

All was well, so long as Wesley and regularly ordained ministers, alone, administered. But as the resentment of the Methodists against immoral clergymen increased, they more and more refused to receive the sacrament from them. This refusal was against the spirit and intention of Article XXVI which said regarding the ministrations of unworthy priests: "Neither is the effect of Christ's ordinance taken away by their wickedness." [11] The Article was formulated to meet the objections of the Anabaptists who separated from the Lord's Table because of *improbitate ministrorum*. When the Church was so outspoken on this doctrine the Methodists could expect little sympathy from it, if they objected to receiving the sacrament from its clergy for reasons similar to those given by the Anabaptists.[12] Then too, other clergymen were accused of singling out the Methodists and refusing to give them communion. Many people went into dissenting churches, or came to the Methodist societies, it was alleged, because they would have the sacrament, but would not receive it from any immoral clergyman.[13] Other laymen who were educated would not stand such treatment. They either stayed away from Church, or, like Joseph Cownley and Thomas Walsh, "occasionally administered the Lord's Supper to the people who were like-minded with themselves, and also to one another." [14]

---
[8] *Sermon, Works*, vol. vii, p. 7.
[9] *Jour.*, vol. vi, p. 59.
[10] *Ibid.*, vol. iv, p. 527.
[11] *Cf.*, Article xxvi.
[12] Charles Hardwick: *History of the Articles of Religion*, p. 104, note 3.
[13] Jackson: *Life of C. Wesley*, p. 524.
[14] *Ibid.*, p. 498.

This migrating of the people from the Church to the Methodist societies put an extra burden upon the preachers so that there were not enough ordained men to administer the Lord's Supper. The people felt this lack keenly; and at Norwich, they urged their preachers to give them the sacrament. These men—Paul Greenwood, John Murlin, and Thomas Mitchell—were not ordained; but they began to administer the sacrament. Charles Wesley summoned these men to London. He wrote to John Wesley, saying that other Methodists were quite ready to take the step which was taken at Norwich, therefore John Wesley should come out in the open and make a decision in this matter. Charles Wesley was quite aroused. He wrote to Nicolas Gilbert, "My soul abhors the thought of separation from the Church of England. You and all the preachers know, if my brother should ever leave it, I should leave him, or rather he me. . . . Indeed, you must become at last either Church ministers or Dissenting." [15] These lay preachers were stopped from administering and Wesley avoided making a decision at this time by serving the communion himself. "I administered the Lord's Supper as usual to the society, and had at least fifty more communicants than this time last year. In the evening, many hundreds went away not being able to squeeze into the room." [16] The people of Norwich still were not adequately furnished with the opportunity to receive the sacrament, while they desired it as much as ever. But Conference was firm and noted that "Mr. Walsh and his friends engaged to desist from the administration of the Lord's Supper." [17] This was a makeshift, not a final settlement.

The clergy, too, had their troubles in connection with this question of the eucharist. They thought the Methodists too particular about receiving the eucharist from certain clergy. They complained that the Methodists came in large numbers to receive communion in churches not their own, putting the minister to great inconvenience because he could not administer to such

---

[15] Jackson: *Life of C. Wesley*, p. 774ff.
[16] *Jour.*, vol. v, p. 487.
[17] Jackson: *Op. cit.*, p. 504.

148 THE SEPARATION OF THE METHODISTS

large numbers properly. He was either obliged to turn these new comers away, or else run the risk of giving the sacrament to strangers unfit to receive it. This was a practical objection and would lead some to infer that the rules of the Church were "not only broken, but notoriously despised by the new sect of Methodists." [18]

Matters were in this unsettled state at the death of Wesley. After his death there was an agitation for greater freedom in receiving the sacraments. In 1792, some Methodists announced: "We are not contending for a general separation of the Methodists from the Church, but for every person in our community to worship God according to the dictates of his own conscience. If any who are with us wish to attend the service of the Church, and receive the sacraments as they have done before, we lay no restraint upon them: they are at full liberty to enjoy what privileges they please with us and go to Church without opposition. If any persons wish to attend any Dissenting Chapel and meet with us as usual, we give them full liberty to do as they think is right before God. Many of our societies cannot go with peaceable mind to the Church for the sacrament. They will either neglect the sacrament or go from us to the Dissenters. All we contend for is, that persons of this determination may have the sacrament from their own preachers." [19] Methodists were becoming tired of the restrictions placed upon them by the Church, and were even becoming friendly with the Dissenters in their desire to receive the sacrament. The situation annoyed them. "Mr. Cownley . . . has preached the gospel upwards of fifty years; . . . this man must refuse the sacrament to his own children, . . . though they entreat him to give it to them with tears; this man, we say, must send them from himself to a drunken parish priest, who neither fears God nor regards man, to have the sacrament 'duly administered to them.'" [20] The Methodists felt the situation intolerable, and insisted that the Church should provide for them better, or else that their own

---

[18] Gibson: *Observation, etc.*, p. 6.
[19] *Address to the Members and friends of the Meth. Soc. in Newcastle*, Intro. pp. v-vi.
[20] *Ibid.*, p. 15.

FROM THE CHURCH OF ENGLAND 149

preachers should give them the sacrament. But the Church remained either hostile or negligent; so the latter happened.

SECTION III. HOURS OF CHURCH SERVICE

The Methodist propaganda was not started to take men out of the Church; but to transform their lives and make them more helpful to the Church. In view of this fact, Wesley would not conduct any of his services at the time when services were taking place in the Established Church. At Athlone, though it was Easter, he preached at three in the afternoon—not during Church hours.[21] At Portarlington, Ireland, he preached at eight and two o'clock.[22] The services in the Church came at another time. Once in Bristol, he preached three times during one Sunday; but never once preached while the services were going on in the Church.[23] At Zennor, as soon as the Church service ended, he preached.[24] Another time "at eleven we went to Church, and heard a plain, useful sermon. At two I preached."[25]

Not only did Wesley refrain from preaching during Church hours; but he attended Church himself and urged his preachers to do so. In Liverpool, he said: "I received much comfort at the old Church in the morning, and at St. Thomas's in the afternoon. It was as if both sermons had been made for me. I pity those who can find no good at Church."[26] And in the *Large Minutes,* the Methodist preachers were directed while in the Church as follows: "Repeat the Lord's Prayer aloud after the minister as often as he says it. Repeat after him aloud every confession, and both doxologies in the communion service. Always kneel during public prayer."[27] Six rules were laid down by the Conference governing the assistants in this matter. They were to: a. exhort all our people to keep close to the Church and sacrament, b. warn them against despising the prayers of

---

[21] *Jour.,* vol. iii, p. 344.
[22] *Ibid.,* vol. iii, p. 408.
[23] *Ibid.,* vol. v, p. 232.
[24] *Ibid.,* vol. iv, p. 408.
[25] *Ibid.,* vol. iii, p. 340.
[26] *Ibid.,* vol. iv, p. 312.
[27] *Works,* vol. v, pp. 224-225.

the Church, c. against calling our society, "The Church," d. against calling our preachers "ministers"; our houses "Meeting-houses"; call them plainly, preaching houses or chapels, e. do not license them as Dissenters.[28] The Methodists intended to worship in the Church and remain in it.

Wesley later, however, modified his position. Coke planned services at Dublin in Whitefriar Street during Church hours for every three Sundays out of four in the month. Wesley said, "We must have no more services at Whitefriars in the Church hours."[29] Later on, however, Wesley wrote a letter to Moore granting such services.[30] And in his sermon on the *Ministerial Office*, he defended his action on the ground that by permitting services during Church hours in Ireland, he prevented separation from the Church.[31]

Methodists were not in hearty accord with Wesley on this matter. In 1774 it was needful to remind the Methodists that Conference had decided that they should attend Church even though the officiating clergyman were not eminent for piety. Grace could be conveyed by wicked ministers; so the Methodists were urged to stay in Church services and get this grace.[32] This argument was not accepted, and in 1781, three preachers wrote to Wesley asking him whether or not they should attend the Church: a. when they heard Calvinism preached, b. when the sermon filled them with prejudice, c. and when they were obliged to tell the people that they did not like the sermon. They asked Wesley to publish his answer. He answered: "If it does not hurt you, hear them; if it does, refrain. Be determined by your own conscience. Let every man in particular act as he is 'persuaded in his own mind.'"[33] An actual change of front on this question took place; for Wesley was fully aware of the state of mind of his preachers. He knew they were but looking for the opportunity to avoid attendance upon the services of the Church.

---

[28] *Works*, vol. v, p. 227.
[29] Tyerman: vol. iii, p. 543.
[30] *Ibid.*, vol. iii, p. 543.
[31] *Sermons, Works*, vol. ii, p. 543.
[32] *Works*, vol. ii, p. 368ff.
[33] *Ibid.*, vol. vii, p. 307.

A year later he was asked if the Methodists should go to Church if the preachers did not preach the truth and frankly admitted that this question troubled him. "I still advise all our friends, when this case occurs, quietly and silently to go out. Only I must earnestly caution them not to be critical; not to make a man an offender by a word; no, nor for a few sentences, which any who believe the decrees may drop without design." Only deliberate attempts to preach untruth should drive Methodists away from the Church service.[34]

The Methodists became bolder when they saw Wesley's line of thinking. In 1786 Dr. Coke suggested to the Conference that in large towns, Methodist services ought to be held in Church hours. "Upon hearing this, Mr. Charles Wesley, with a very loud voice and in great anger, cried out, 'No,' which was the only word he uttered during the whole of the Conference sittings," Mr. Mather, undaunted, confirmed what Coke had said.[35] The people at Deptford also urged Wesley to allow Sunday service in the room at the time of Church service. But Wesley clearly saw that to allow this, would be to allow and encourage separation, and that this was not only inexpedient, but also quite unlawful for him to do.[36] He therefore would not permit this change of hours, though he had openly ordained. The people still stayed in the chapel at Deptford, he recorded, even though he did not change the time of service.[37] But this constant desire of his people, tended continually to modify Wesley's attitude, and in 1786, Conference permitted services during Church hours in Yorkshire under the following conditions:

    a. When the minister is a notoriously wicked man.

    b. When he preaches Arian or any equally pernicious doctrine.

    c. When there are not churches in the town sufficient to contain half the people.

    d. When there is no Church at all within two or three miles.[38]

---

[34] *Ibid.*, vol. vii, p. 308.
[35] Tyerman: vol. iii, p. 478.
[36] *Jour.*, vol. vii, p. 217.
[37] *Ibid.*, vol. vii, p. 241.
[38] *Minutes*, vol. i, p. 191.

This was a compromise, and with this question not settled, Wesley died.

Insufficiency of church accommodation was an important factor at this time. The testimony of James Alan Park, afterwards a justice of the Common Pleas, and others, would bear out the contention of the Methodists. In 1814 Park wrote to Bishop Howley of the See of London saying, that the want of opportunity for public worship he believed to be "one great cause of the apparent defection from the Church, and of the increase of Sectarism and Methodism". The rapid shifting of the population caused by the rise of industry in the eighteenth century had not been met by the Church. New parishes were not created in the industrial centers, while the old parishes were too poorly equipped to meet the needs of the dense population. It was not until 1818 that the Church became sufficiently aroused over this need to meet it by founding the *Church Building Society* with the Archbishop of Canterbury as its president, and the king as one of its chief patrons. But when this step was taken to supply the necessary churches the Methodist movement had been well launched and already counted as of Dissent. The time to organize the *Church Building Society* was when Wesley was alive. This might have kept his followers within the Established Church. But the Church was not farsighted enough to do this.[39]

The Conference of 1788 had ruled that: "The assistants shall have discretionary power to read the prayer-book in the preaching houses on Sunday mornings, where they think it expedient, if the generality of the society acquiesce with it; on condition that Divine service never be performed in the Church hours on the Sundays when the sacrament is administered in the parish Church, where the preaching house is situated, and the people be strenuously exhorted to attend the sacrament in the parish Church on these Sundays".[40] In other words: Services could be held in Church hours when communion was not to be given. This was a concession on the part of Conference; but the people

---

[39] Stephens and Hunt: *History of the Eng. Church*, vol. viii, pt. i, pp. 77-79.
[40] *Minutes*, vol. i, p. 208.

FROM THE CHURCH OF ENGLAND 153

were not satisfied. Samuel Bradburn took this matter up and reviewed the history of this question and Wesley's decisions in detail. "He changed the time of service in the Foundry from being early in the morning only, on Sundays as well as other days, to Church hours on Sundays in the forenoon. And notwithstanding the insignificance of this change, it was the real source of every alteration that followed . . . the generality of the people did not consider it as dissenting from the Church, though they had no more to do with the Church, as to real connection or subordination, than with the Jews." [41] In this way Bradburn traced the development of this subject and urged that services be held unconditionally in Church hours. At Salford, Bradburn did change the time of the Methodist services from eight to ten o'clock, and called it "crossing the Rubicon." [42]

Thus the Methodists had turned in their practice. They no longer urged their people in a most solemn manner to attend the Church service every Sunday. The matter was being reversed. Many of them were holding their own services at hours identical with those of service in the Church and this made the former position untenable. It indicated the growth of a new and different kind of spirit in Methodism—a spirit hostile toward the Established Church.

SECTION IV. THE CONFUSION AFTER WESLEY'S DEATH

With nothing definitely settled regarding the Lord's Supper, and with no out and out ruling by Conference permitting services in Church hours, Methodism faced a complex situation. Wesley had died. No sooner was he buried, than the Methodists were deluged with pamphlets urging strict conformity with the Established Church.[43] This question eventually had to be settled. Some were beginning to object to the way in which Methodism was being conducted. They did not like the idea of having one hundred men control the Conference. Coke had previously pointed out that this was giving the one hundred men too much power, while Wesley himself seemed to have sympathized with

---
[41] Bradburn: *The Question: Are Methodists Dissenters?* p. 11.
[42] W. H. S. *Proceedings*, vol. i, p. 42-43.
[43] Myles: *Chronological History of the People Called Methodists*, p. 208.

Coke's criticism.[44] Many made an attempt to nullify the *Deed of Declaration* which legally incorporated these one hundred men into the Conference; but in vain. At the same time, others felt that "the moment that the *Deed* was superseded, there would have been an end of the Wesleyan itineracy and order." They were afraid of more democracy.[45] Of Wesley's influence, some of the preachers thought that it fell to the Conference, some of the trustees thought that it fell to them, and Mr. Kilham and his friends thought that it fell to the people at large.[46] The executors of Wesley's will added to this complexity, for they reported that they must still keep control over Wesley's property and that they would not give it to the Conference.[47] Many were the crosscurrents of opinion and feeling that were threatening Methodism at this crucial time.

To increase this confusion, such productions as an *Address to the Members and Friends of the Methodist Society in Newcastle* was distributed which said, "Whoever reads what Mr. [Charles] Wesley published, will easily perceive, he did not think always alike respecting the Church of England."[48] Bradburn told troubled Methodists that he had heard him say, he should be afraid to meet his father's spirit in paradise if he left the Church. Then of his brother: "Mr. John Wesley, on the other hand, as we have seen, remained therein with a doubting conscience."[49] The whole question of whether the Methodists were Dissenters, was raised. "If clergymen were persecuted for truth and driven out of the Church, as Mr. Wesley and his brother were, we are ready to receive them with open arms; but when they leave the Church of their own accord . . . they are more Dissenters than any of the Methodist preachers, and whether designedly so or not, they are in reality sapping the very foundations of the Church."[50] This treatise further quoted Wesley with saying, "As soon as I am dead, the Methodists will

---
[44] Myles: p. 201.
[45] Jackson: *Cent. of Wes. Meth.*, p. 159.
[46] Myles: p. vii.
[47] *Ibid.*, p. 207.
[48] Intro., p. iv.
[49] *The Question*, p. 10.
[50] *Ibid.*, p. 12.

FROM THE CHURCH OF ENGLAND

be a regular Presbyterian Church."[51] Indeed, a kind of separation had already taken place, it urged, because people stayed away from the Church on account of a bad vicar, and they never returned.[52]

Coke very boldly said that many of the people would have separated from the Church long ago, had it not been for the superior wisdom of Wesley, and assumed that all were ready to separate.[53] Methodists were far from being unanimously inclined to separate. Wesley was gone. They were confused, and did not know how to act in unison.

In this confusion Conference was able to assemble in 1791, and the men whose names were enrolled in the *Deed of Declaration* voted by ballot for a president and secretary.[54] A moderately inclined man, William Thompson, was elected president.[55] Conference was able to pull itself together and made rules governing the office of president. In 1792 it ruled that a president could not succeed himself, and could not be elected oftener than once in eight years, for his power ceased at the close of Conference.[56] The Conference of 1793 gave all preachers who had travelled fourteen years, additional rights.[57] But even this work was bitterly attacked and the president of the Conference was called a *generalissimo*. The movement was compared with that of Loyola and said to be just as dangerous; Conference was a pure hierarchy; its members did not have equal rights; its ministers were mere puppets; the one hundred who could vote were an *imperium in imperio*.[58]

A little of the work of organization was also done in spite of this confusion of program resulting from the death of Wesley. The whole of Methodism in the three kingdoms was divided into twenty-seven districts. Each assistant had charge of a district, with the power to summon the preachers of his district in

---

[51] *Ibid.*, pp. 18-19.
[52] *Ibid.*, p. 15.
[53] *Sermon on Asbury's Ordination*, p. 10.
[54] Myles: p. 197.
[55] Stevens: *Op. cit.*, vol. iii, p. 33.
[56] *Minutes*, vol. i, p. 259.
[57] Warren: vol. i, p. 102.
[58] Beard: *Rise . . . of Methodism*, p. 5ff.

156 THE SEPARATION OF THE METHODISTS

full connection, for any critical occasion. The preachers so summoned, met and chose a chairman and could make decisions that were final until the following Conference. Nothing, however, could be done contrary to a previous ruling of Conference.[59] In each district there were to be not less than three, nor more than eight circuits.[60] The Conference of 1791 authorized a committee, composed of one member elected by every district in the three kingdoms, and this committee was to provide a plan for stationing the preachers.[61] Those whom Wesley had authorized in his will to preach and appoint preachers for the New Chapel in City Road, and King Street Chapel in Bath, signed an agreement that they would work in an entire subservience to the Conference.[62]

Thus far was the program and reorganization of the work carried in peace. But so great was the confusion, so varied the ideas of what ought to be done, so strong the contention, that no further progress was made without turmoil and strife. Those who wished to remain within the Established Church were shocked at the suggestions made in the various pamphlets. Those who wished to be free from the restraints and oversights of the Church, stood for greater changes than had taken place or were suggested.

Section V. Party Struggle and the Sacrament

There were two parties at work with their programs in Methodism. The radical party advocated that Conference should not only ordain, but have a definite rule about it. It accused Conference of avoiding this entire question of ordination.[63] This party felt that Conference had the entirely wrong view of the matter of the sacrament. The decision of the Conference of 1793 was attacked; because it made a minister go out to his people and urge them not to take the sacrament, but if the people insisted they could receive it from their preachers. This

---

[59] *Minutes*, vol. i, p. 241.
[60] Myles: p. 211.
[61] *Minutes*, vol. i, p. 247.
[62] Warren: vol. i, p. 51.
[63] Paul and Silas: *Earnest Address* . . . p. 22.

attitude of the Conference encouraged the people to go without the sacrament.[64] But when Conference decided *by lot*, whether it would permit its preachers to use the sacrament for one year, the wrath of this party knew no bounds. "After much wrangling and debate, God Almighty suffered the Conference to enter into a temptation, which will disgrace Methodism to the end of the world. . . . One of the best men we have in our connection out of zeal for peace, tempted the Conference to decide by lot, what was self evident. Lots ought never to be used, but where it is impossible to do without them." One Isaac Brown ran out of Conference crying shame when this was done. Many of the Conference would not vote at all; yet the minutes read: "All were satisfied. All submitted." They insisted that the minutes contained what was not true and that this was no statesmanlike way of settling such a question.[65]

The radicals were also opposed to the domination of the trustees over the worship of the Methodists. The people should worship as they saw fit and not be controlled by a minority of trustees. "The Conference had better allow the people this privilege freely, as have it extorted from them." The trustees should be treated with respect; but they should not be allowed to hinder the people from worshiping as they saw fit.[66] Furthermore, to follow Wesley, was not to stay in the Church regardless of any result. To follow Wesley's plan would mean: to ordain; to wear gowns and bands if necessary; to have services in Church hours if found useful; to make an avowed separation if good people required it; in fact this party cared for no manner of compromise.[67]

To offset this party and balk it in its work, there was the conservative group. This party worked hard to steer a middle course and stated: "The Methodists as a community are not, and with propriety cannot be strictly either Church people or Dissenters; but a society 'whose only bond of unity is piety,' and that admits indiscriminately Churchmen, Dissenters, or what

---

[64] *Ibid.*, p. 8.
[65] *Ibid.*, p. 6.
[66] Paul and Silas: *Op. cit.*, p. 17.
[67] *Ibid.*, p. 5.

else, provided they give Scriptural proofs; desire to flee from the wrath to come. We have no rule which requires our people to belong either to the Church or to the Dissenters."[68] These conservatives saw clearly that Methodism was at a crisis. They conscientiously sought to steer the *via media,* and yet to lean toward a strong power on Conference, feeling in this crisis that it would not be well for the people to have too much power, for this would lead to temptation and corruption. Conference was not put in the way of this temptation, whereas the people were, therefore the conservatives would pay no attention to Kilham, and worked for a strong centralization of power in Conference.[69] This party had much influence with the Conference inasmuch as it proposed granting large powers to that body, and under its influence the Conference of 1792 dealt with the matters of Church hours, the checking of enthusiasm, etc., in a compromising manner. It ruled that "no ordination shall take place in the Methodist connection without the consent of the Conference first obtained," and anyone who broke this rule was thereby automatically excluded from the Conference.[70] This action was taken in the face of requests that the Conference give greater liberties to ordain. The Conference of 1793 also showed the influence of this party. It ruled "that no gowns, cassocks, bands, surplices, shall be worn by any of the preachers." Even the title "Reverend" was not to be used by any of the preachers. Yet the distinction between ordained and unordained preachers was to be dropped.[71] This action, taken in 1793, was reaffirmed in the Conference of the following year. Conference ruled that it still did not desire the use of the title "Reverend"; preaching in Church hours was not permitted only for special reasons, and then "when it will not cause a division among the people"; the preachers were "not to baptize only when it was to promote peace and concord."[72] This shows that this conservative party was strong and that it had much influence with the Conference

---

[68] Crowther: *Crisis of Methodism,* p. 6.
[69] *Ibid., Christian Order, passim.*
[70] *Minutes,* vol. i, pp. 259-260.
[71] *Ibid.,* pp. 277-278.
[72] *Ibid.,* p. 299.

in putting its policies into effect. The struggle within Methodism over the matter of the sacraments, was actually a struggle taking place between the radicals and the conservatives.

Stevens said that Wesley had been dead no longer than two months before the question of the sacrament came to the front. Laymen of Hull, Birmingham, and Sheffield, issued a protest against it in print.[73] The reason given for this was that "a large proportion of Methodists had been Dissenters, and were whether conscientiously or whimsically unwilling to resort to the national Church for the sacraments."[74] This does explain one of the real causes for the disturbance within Methodism over the question of the sacraments; but the underlying reason for the rise of this question was the fact that it had never been definitely settled while Wesley was alive. In 1792 the uneasiness respecting this matter increased throughout Methodism, for the people missed the sacraments which John Wesley was wont to administer to them when he preached. Some preachers wished to furnish this need, others thought it unwise; so the question was brought into the foreground.[75]

Every Methodist knew that separation from the Church was an actual fact in theory and practice as soon as the Methodists could freely have the sacrament in their own meeting houses. The Conference of 1792 therefore decided: "The Lord's Supper shall not be administered by any person among our societies in England and Ireland; for the ensuing year, on any consideration whatsoever."[76] There was so little unity about this matter, that the above decision was reached only by drawing the above mentioned lot. Adam Clarke sought thereby to settle the matter, but it was merely a poor attempt to compromise.[77] As a result of this, the Conference of 1793 was obliged to say frankly that it faced a dilemma. Some wished to keep the sacrament out of the chapels in accord with the ruling of the previous Conference, others threatened to leave the Methodists if they

---

[73] Vol. iii, p. 27.
[74] *Ibid.*
[75] Myles: p. 219.
[76] *Minutes*, p. 260.
[77] *Ibid.*, p. 263.

did not have these sacraments. To meet this situation the Conference again sought a compromise by moving: "that the sacrament of the Lord's Supper shall not be administered by the preachers in any part of our connection, except where the whole society is unanimous for it, and will not be content without it; and even in those few exempt societies, it shall be administered as far as practical, in the evening only, and according to the form of the Church of England. For we could not bear that the sacrament which was instituted by our Lord as a bond of peace and union should become a bone of contention."[78] Conference was evidently being forced by some of the churches, yet tried to make it appear that the minority of Methodists were forcing it to make this concession. But minorities do not force legislative bodies alone; they can do so only with the help of the majority. The people, in fact, had become used to having the sacraments, and they did not like the action of the previous Conference taking them away from them. Conference at this time frankly said, "it is the people . . . who have forced us into this deviation from our union with the Church of England."[79] This "deviation" was a conscious separation.

The Conference of 1793 was a compromise as well as the one before it; hence one is not surprised to see that the practice of administering the communion was reported to have extended to 48 circuits and 108 chapels in the Conference of 1794.[80] Many had availed themselves of the provisions granted by the Conference of 1793. In 1795, Sutcliffe, a member of the liberal party, came out with a strong argument for a greater liberty in this matter. He brought forward the old argument of the dissipation, debauchery, fraud, and revelings of the clergy as a reason for non-attendance upon the sacrament.[81] He said: "Yet after the nicest calculation, I question whether more than 5,000 of 60,000 English Methodists regularly receive communion in the Established Church . . . there are more than 50,000 who live almost in neglect of this sacred and solemn institution"—

---

[78] *Minutes*, vol. i, pp. 279-280.
[79] *Ibid.*, vol. i, p. 280.
[80] *Ibid.*, pp. 294-295.
[81] *Christian Liberty*, p. 9.

this being the case, Conference must provide for this need in the Church.[82] The Methodists were too poor to own sittings in the Church, and when they crowded large churches to hear good sermons they were ordered out when it came time for the communion. The clergy did not want Methodists at their communion services.[83] These were the reasons why the Methodists should be at full liberty to have their own communion services. A wide and sympathetic hearing was given to all argumentation of this nature. The determination of the Methodists was increasing.

Conference was finally obliged to note the trend of sentiment, and in 1796 it gave the district superintendents accurate instructions in regard to the communion. Each society that wished the sacrament should have it. If the superintendent would not give it, he had to supply a properly qualified preacher who would. No preacher was to urge his people to have this communion; neither was he to keep it from them. They were to be left free to decide upon this matter as they wished.[84] This arrangement had all the marks of a *bona fide* separation. The people could do as they pleased about separating. The outcome of this one can see in the *Plan of Pacification*, which was brought forward in 1795.

SECTION VI. TRUSTEEISM AND THE METHODIST NEW CONNECTION

As the struggle raged between the radicals and the conservative party in regard to the sacrament, so did the struggle wax warm between these same parties in regard to the position in Methodism of trustees of property. Conference had none too good an opinion of the trustees, for in a circular letter of 1793, it said that there were disloyal trustees who did not adequately support Methodist work, but rather bred discontent by holding sittings in Dissenting meeting houses. Conferences suspected them of desiring to get all power into their hands.[85]

---

[82] *Op. cit.*, p. 8.
[83] *Op. cit.*, p. 13.
[84] Warren: vol. i, p. 151.
[85] *Minutes*, vol. i, p. 281ff.

Feeling at this time ran high as was evidenced by the tone of this letter. Conference thought of these men as having tendencies toward the Dissenters. Abel Stevens called them the "high-church lay-aristocracy of Methodism."[86] And the later actions of these, he characterized as: "a blow at the fundamental plan of Methodism; and generally followed, it would have destroyed the itinerant system by subjecting the pulpit to local control."[87] Both of these opposite views do not deny but that trusteeism tended to destroy the feeling of unity which made Methodism such a movement as it was.

This tense feeling came to an expression when the trustees ousted Henry Moore, a preacher ordained by Wesley, from a Methodist chapel in Bristol; because he had not been appointed to the said chapel by them.[88] Just previous to this action they had requested Conference for the right to sit with that body, and to decide with it regarding the administration of the sacrament; but Conference did not let these trustees become a part of itself; instead, it sought to compromise the matter and to do this, issued rules governing the actions of the trustees.[89] The principle involved in this action of the trustees was twofold: it was a question of the extent of the power of the Conference, and it was a question of further deviation from the Church. "The Conference may be assured that the Bristol trustees desire most earnestly to *concur* with them in the appointment of preachers for this circuit," but the trustees advised Conference to send only able men, for no others would be acceptable. This was the attitude of the trustees, while Conference insisted upon the subordination of the trustees to its will.[90] Yet the trustees added that it was not a question of whether the trustees controlled or not; but rather a question of whether Henry Moore should turn into Dissenters the society of Bristol; of whom nineteen out of twenty were members of the Established Church. The consciousness of separation from the

---

[86] Vol. iii, p. 53.
[87] *Ibid.*, p. 57.
[88] Myles: p. 227ff.
[89] *Ibid.*, p. 225ff.
[90] Trustees of Bristol: *Primitive Methodism Defended*, p. 5.

Church was present in the reasonings of the trustees. They further added: "It was the divine will we should be auxiliaries to, and not separatists from the Established Church. Consequently, we cannot permit the ordinances of baptism or the Lord's Supper to be administered among us by our own preachers, nor having preachers in our chapels during the time of divine service in the Church."[91] The trustees did not want further separation, in this instance, while the people did.

The preachers, and those who believed in supporting the powers of Conference, and who were not overcareful of the good will of the Established Church, bitterly attacked the trustees of Bristol for putting Moore out of their chapel. Benjamin Rhodes, a Methodist writer of the times, was exceedingly violent, and in his attack upon these trustees, severely handled them. His attack was upon three points:

1. Shall trustees in the Methodist connection place and displace preachers at their pleasure? or, shall they not?
2. Shall Methodist preachers aid trustees that claim such power? or, shall they not?
3. Shall we suffer a combination of trustees and others to overturn old Methodism? or, shall we not?[92]

Longridge put the matter strongly by saying: "If any man on account of his property, influence, wisdom, or piety, arrogate a power to compel the consciences of others in their duty to God, he precisely resembles him who exalteth himself above all that is called God. It is probable that our brethren are not aware of these consequences." And further, he stated that these trustees used the same principles as did the pope.[93] All of Methodism was aroused over this question.

After Moore was ousted, he became very polemic and attacked the trustees in a pamphlet entitled, *A Reply to a Pamphlet Entitled Considerations on a Separation of the Methodists from the Established Church.* Moore said that in practice there had been separation from the Church in the societies of London

---

[91] *Ibid.*, p. 14.
[92] Rhodes: *The Point Stated*, p. 4.
[93] *Conciliatory Essay*, p. 21.

for the last forty years, "yet there is properly no separation from the Church in London—no independent Church formed. Every one that pleases may, as in Bristol, attend his parish Church. Meantime the Church Service is read every Lord's day, without any regard to any other worshiping body of people. The Lord's Supper is administered in them all."[94] Moore was clear-headed enough to see that separation was a fact, not a theory. After this general statement, he came at the trustees with the following: "That men professing to be Methodists should expel a preacher, appointed by the Conference, from those chapels, against the mind of the leaders, stewards, and people, without any charge preferred, or trial of any kind, taking counsel only with their attorney, is rather new in the religious world: And everyone that knows what Methodism is, must know that such conduct tends to its dissolution."[95]

The trustees were not inclined to be conciliatory; but continued their demands for representation in the Conference. They were put off with good words; but their agitations brought upon the whole connection the *Plan of Pacification,* in which Conference gained the victory, and the anti-separating trustees lost.[96] "The result of the struggle was most salutary, not only in the restoration of harmony, but, if possible, more so, as giving a consolidated government to Wesleyan Methodism."[97] Had this attempt of the trustees to set aside the *Deed of Declaration* succeeded, "Methodist societies would have been converted into Independent churches," and the whole of the Methodist plan would have fallen through.[98] But this attempt came to nought.

The trustees openly claimed to support the conservative ideas of Methodism.[99] In fact, they were so ultra-conservative that even the conservative Conference opposed them. Yet it is unique that these ultra-conservatives were backed up in their demands by the radicals. Alexander Kilham was the leader of these radicals. As early as 1791 he issued a circular in which

---

[94] *Op. cit.,* p. 5.
[95] H. Moore: *Op. cit.,* p. 8.
[96] Myles: p. 229.
[97] Stevens: *Op. cit.,* vol. iv, p. 73.
[98] Jackson: *Cent. of Wes. Meth.,* pp. 158-159.
[99] Trustees of Bristol: *Op. cit.,* p. 14.

he made war on all who wished to remain in the Church. This came out just before Conference time and made a stir.[100] But the Conference took no notice of this attack and appointed him to Newcastle, where he found the societies split upon the sacramental question. To meet the situation, Kilham would not compromise; but published a pamphlet in which he advocated that the people should decide as they saw fit. The Conference of 1792 rebuked him for his "impolitic" pamphlet.[101] Kilham supported the trustees in so far as they were in the opposition; but his principles were different from theirs. He did not wish the power of Methodism to be vested in the Conference; but neither did he wish it to be vested in the trustees. He was a thoroughgoing democrat, and wished the power to be vested in the people. The people, not the Conference, should control. For advocating this, he was expelled from Methodism in 1796, after a regular trial.[102] Kilham was antagonistic; he had spoken of a ruling of Conference as a "Methodist Bull," and such speech was not quieting to people who still remembered a certain Bishop Lavington.[103] Kilham was also quite opposed to the compromising attitude of Conference in respect to the sacrament. He said that Conference was inconsistent in permitting it to be administered in some places, while forbidding it in others. This was "priestly domination."

The minority of the people demanded equal lay representation in the Conference, and even brought in a plan for such equality at the district and quarterly meetings. In 1797 all of these plans were vetoed by the Conference, and these people felt obliged to form the *New Connection*.[104] Stephen Eversfield and William Thom refused to sign a declaration of Conference in 1797, and were forced to go along with Kilham.[105] Thus Kilham with his refusal to compromise, with his definite program, with his truly democratic ideas, was forced out. Wesleyan Methodism could ill afford to lose this democratic force thus

---

[100] Stevens: vol. iii, p. 32.
[101] *Ibid.*, vol. iii, p. 40.
[102] Myles: p. 235.
[103] Stevens: vol. iii, p. 65.
[104] *Apology for the New Connection*, pp. 10 and 14.
[105] Myles: p. 242.

represented within the number of her members. But by this opposition, those who wished the people to control, compelled the Conference to become more definite, and less compromising. Conference was compelled to step down from the fence, even though so doing meant further estrangement from the Established Church.

Thus far, we have seen the struggle over the sacrament, in which Conference sought to compromise, and the struggle with trusteeism, which has not at this point been settled. By anticipation we have seen the advocates for a broader democracy lose their fight while a conservative, compromising Conference still held sway. But this sway was over a shaky type of Methodism. It was a Methodism made of individuals, both solicitous and careless regarding the Church. Those careless about the Church were constantly increasing. Faction was spread. Methodism divided against herself could not survive. We must now consider the method adopted to reconcile the warring factions and unite Methodism, though completing the rupture with the Established Church.

SECTION VII. PLAN OF PACIFICATION AND REGULATIONS OF LEEDS

The leaders of Methodism at last became thoroughly aroused to the dangers of the situation.[106] Moore, the advocate of the power of Conference, and Bradburn, who was inclined to favor the trustees, met at the breakfast table of Benson, a prominent leader. Here Thomas Coke visited them. They made mutual concessions and the resulting document was afterward called *The Plan of Pacification*.[107]

This "plan" dealt first with the sacrament. The sacrament was not to be administered in any chapel unless the trustees, stewards, and leaders, as representatives of the people, favored the use of it by a majority. If there was not a chapel, then the decision rested with the leaders and stewards.[108] This same method was to be used in ascertaining whether or not the people

---
[106] *Minutes*, vol. i, p. 321ff.
[107] Stevens: vol. iii, p. 58.
[108] *Minutes*, vol. i, p. 322.

FROM THE CHURCH OF ENGLAND   167

wished service in Church hours, or their preachers to baptize or bury their dead. The Lord's Supper could not, however, be withdrawn from the people when once it had been granted to them. And none but preachers appointed by the Conference could so administer the sacrament. To appease those who were against separation, the "plan" provided that the Lord's Supper should be celebrated only according to the rite of the Established Church. And furthermore, to see that this question was settled once and for all, the "plan" concluded by ordering: that if any local preacher, steward, or leader should disturb the peace of any society by advocating or objecting to the use of the sacrament, he should be tried, and if found guilty, expelled from Methodism.[109]

This plan was in a sense a compromise; but yet it did actually and officially indorse: the services out of Church hours; the administration of the baptism and the Lord's Supper; and most important of all, it distinctly provided against the returning to the old order. If the people of any vicinity once chose to offend the Established Church, Methodism gave them no way of avoiding the giving of this offense a second time. This was actual separation.

The "plan" also dealt with the question of trusteeism. It said: "The appointment of preachers shall remain solely with the Conference; and no trustee, or number of trustees, shall expel or exclude from their chapel or chapels, any preachers so appointed."[110] Trustees could not control Methodism. A way, nevertheless, was provided, so that any preacher inefficient, or immoral, could be temporarily removed until Conference should meet and investigate the preacher in question. But the control of the preachers rested with the Conference and the "plan" distinctly said that if the trustees expelled any preacher of their own *separate* authority, the Conference after proving such a fact, would expel the offending trustees from Methodism and use their chapel no more, but build a new one.[111] In this way, the power

---

[109] *Ibid.*, p. 325.
[110] *Ibid.*, p. 323.
[111] *Ibid.*, p. 324.

of the trustees was denied, and the power of the Conference to conduct the affairs of Methodism vindicated.

The *Plan of Pacification* was adopted by the Conference of 1795. The trustees in a letter to Conference agreed to abide "cheerfully" by the decision of the Conference in this matter. Thus was the strife between the trustees and the Conference settled, while unity again came to its own in Methodism, leaving Conference as the victorious party. The matter of the Lord's Supper was thus settled in such a way as forbade any true harmony between the Methodists and the Established Church. When Conference adopted the *Plan of Pacification,* it did away with any pretense of subserviency to the wishes of the clergy and the Established Church.

In this was the "plan" a real pacification between the conservative and the ultra-conservative party. But what of the radical party represented by Kilham and his followers? This "plan" made no attempt to make peace with the radical party, but rather, it ignored the radicals when they protested, and then drove them out of the connection. Democracy, as we understand it, was not present in this "plan." It was purely a victory for the Conference as over against the trustees on the one hand, and those who wished the people to rule, on the other. Methodism would have done a far wiser thing, had she kept the radical party within her fold.

After the adoption of the *Plan of Pacification,* others, besides Alexander Kilham and his radicals, still troubled the Conference. There was much uneasiness among the Methodists. Kilham still demanded lay-representation; but it was felt that this was not adapted for so large a body, and that it would incapacitate the Conference.[112] When, in 1797, this was refused, the radicals left the Wesleyan Methodists and formed the Methodist New Connection. The Conference feared that many more might leave and follow Kilham. For this reason, it was compelled to modify somewhat its independent attitude, and outline its powers and purposes.[113] The Lord's Supper, baptism, and

---

[112] *Apology for the New Connection,* part iii.
[113] Myles: p. 243.

ordination were to continue, the new Church was not to be forsaken, but Conference was to be more conciliatory. These modifications were called *The Regulations of Leeds*. The need for these regulations shows the lack of complete harmony among the Methodists.

Many of the older men signed *The Regulations of Leeds*. To offset the accusations that the old men in the form of a party machine were controlling Conference, the younger men put forth a statement asserting their satisfaction with the state of affairs and their desire to stay in the connection, insisting that no ecclesiastical aristocracy existed.[114] This would seem to show that within the Conference itself harmony and peace was on the increase. The adoption of these *regulations* did away with most of the uneasiness within Methodism.

Methodism was now, after all of this controversy, more of a unit than it was before Wesley's death. Its internal strife had eliminated all who would cause defection. Only loyal and more or less satisfied members remained within its ranks. But as a result of this strife, it was no longer an integral part of the Church of England. That movement, which had begun early to develop an organization for furthering certain doctrines and practices, now was more solid than ever in advocating even more distinct practices. In spite of strife, Methodism emerged claiming and practicing the right to ordain, bury the dead, and administer the sacraments within its own organization. It did not now claim, as when Wesley was alive, that it was a part of the Established Church. It knew differently. The Established Church had failed to take advantage of a movement that comes extremely rarely to any institution. It had opposed, and neglected Methodism, and done so to its own hurt.

Methodism realized that it was an independent entity. It laid down rules for its dissatisfied members.[115] It strongly urged the purchasing of land upon which to build its chapels.[116] It established its preachers' fund upon a more substantial and more

---

[114] *Minutes*, vol. i, p. 360ff.
[115] *Ibid.*, pp. 346-347.
[116] Warren: *Op. cit.*, p. 260.

workable basis.[117] And in 1808, its Conference openly sought to fix its doctrines; and adopted and established the *Twenty-five Articles of Religion.*[118] It actually was an independent Church. "Any organization organized for carrying on a particular activity, or for achieving some special social end, is a constituent society."[119] Sociologically, Methodism had fulfilled all the requirements of this definition. She was fully organized. Her social end was clearly outlined in her doctrines, Articles of Religion, and elsewhere. This was a constituent society. Opposition met within herself and without, had transformed her "consciousness of kind" into the more solid and distinct realization that she was an independent society—and therefore no part of the Established Church.

---

[117] Myles: p. 221.
[118] W. H. S. *Publications,* No. 2, 1897.
[119] Giddings: *Op. cit.,* p. 501.

CONCLUSION

The separation of the Methodists from the Church of England was a real separation. The large majority of the Methodists, in the beginning, were members of the Church of England. To be sure, there were some Dissenters among their numbers; but in most localities they constituted a very small proportion of the whole. The authorities upon the history of Dissent, say almost nothing about the numbers of Dissenters who joined the Methodist movement, indicating that the number was small enough to be quite ignored.[1] Without any proof, one is conservative in estimating that less than one tenth of the Methodists came out of the ranks of the Dissenters. Primarily, Methodism was not a movement among Dissenters.

Wesley ever claimed to be a good Churchman and that his societies were composed of members of the Church. "We are not Dissenters in the only way our law allows, namely, those who renounce the service of the Church. We do not, dare not separate from it. . . . What they do in America, or what their minutes say on that subject, is nothing to us. We will keep in the good old way."[2] Professor Faulkner, nevertheless quite correctly says: "But, as a matter of fact, Wesley had in effect separated himself from the Church."[3] To be sure, the Methodists would not take advantage of the Act of Toleration.[4] But this refusal was not due to a loyal desire to adhere to the Church, and John Free objected to them on this very score, that they were in reality Dissenters, and yet refused to register themselves as such.[5]

The Church too, considered the Methodists in their early days as a part of itself. Bishop Gibson objected to the whole of the Methodist organization, categorically taking up each point,

---

[1] *Vide* Waddington, Ivimey, Bouge and Bennett, Wilson.
[2] *Works, Large Minutes,* vol. v, p. 227.
[3] *Papers of Am. Soc. of Ch. Hist.,* 1st series, vol. viii, 1897, p. 175.
[4] Tyerman: vol. iii, pp. 512-513.
[5] *Sermon of 1758.*

such as: exhorters, bands, societies, and denied that they were legal or warranted in the law. Such criticism would not apply to out-and-out Dissenters. Thus both Wesley and Churchmen in the early days considered the Methodists as part of the Church.

Wesley's idea, however, was to found a society within the Church of England with rules, organization, and discipline and even in a sense, a doctrinal emphasis all its own. According to the law there could be no such society, for the parish was the unit, and all such bodies made a church within a church. This was schismatical from the standpoint of legalism. The attitude of Bishop Gibson was the purely legal one. If a Churchman built a meeting house, he defied the law and the only way of legalizing such a meeting house was to declare it a chapel under the Toleration Act. One could not be a Churchman with a private conventicle such as the Methodists habitually held. To persist in this line was to be a Dissenter. The Churchmen were quite independent, sadly shortsighted, shamefully illiberal; but their position was legal. When the spirit of Methodism broke with the spirit of legalism within the Church, Methodists became Dissenters.

"The question of the separation of the Methodists from the Church of England was a question in perpetual discussion in the Conferences from the first Conference almost to the close of Wesley's life." [6] This showed a growing antipathy toward the Church. Some of the preachers wished for a separation and worked hard for it.[7] Wesley maintained the upper hand and kept these in the Church.[8] Had the Methodists considered themselves *not* members of the Church, and had their enemies considered them not to be members of the Church, then there would never have been this discussion. One is safe in thinking that a large majority of the Methodists were members of the Church of England when Wesley died. After the terms of the *Plan of Pacification* and *The Regulations of Leeds* went into effect, one is not correct in thinking that either temperamentally or sociolog-

---

[6] Faulkner: *Op. cit.*, p. 174.
[7] Charles Wesley: *Journal,* vol. ii, p. 134.
[8] *Jour.*, vol. vii, p. 192 and vol. vi, p. 203, vol. iv, pp. 186 and 422.

ically the Methodists were part of the Established Church. There was, to be sure, no formal declaration of the severance of relationships with the Established Church; but the separation was an accomplished fact.

When the discipline of the parent church was defied, and when an admirable and distinct organization was formed, the destiny of the Methodists was to separate.[9] If Wesley and his followers had not been thrust out of the Church, the very spirit and power of their movement, the nature of the work to be done, the somewhat unusual methods which they were compelled to adopt for its accomplishment would have taken them out. They were of the Church neither by adoption nor by spirit.[10] But this separation was not in vain, for the movement contributed more to the reviving of religion among the lower classes of England than any other since the days of the Friars, while up to the present it has carried, as widely as Christianity is known, its message for the moral transformation of the individual and for the reformation of society.

---

[9] *Cf.* W. E. H. Lecky: *Op. cit.*, vol. ii, p. 688.
[10] *Vide*, Fitchett: p. 180.

BIBLIOGRAPHY

Libraries Consulted

Columbia University Library.
Drew Theological Seminary Library has many good secondary works, many pamphlets, and contains the Tyerman Collection which is rich in the material of Methodism for the 18th century.
General Theological Seminary Library holds many Methodist works; but is especially rich in about 150 volumes of anti-Methodistical publications known as the Cavender Collection.
Union Theological Seminary Library contains helps to bibliography, many periodicals, biographies, pamphlets, and secondary works.

Bibliographical Helps

Archbald, F. A. Methodism and Literature. Cincinnati, 1883.
Brown, William. Wesleyan Methodism—a catalogue of books. London, (after 1826).
Cavender, Curtis H. Catalogue of Work in Refutation of Methodism, from its Origin, 1729 to the Present Time. . . . New York, 1868. 2nd ed.
Green, Richard. Anti-Methodist Publications Issued During the 18th Century. London, 1902.
Green, Richard. The Works of John and Charles Wesley. A Bibliography. London, 1906.
Jackson, Francis M. Index to Library Edition to Thomas Jackson's Life of Charles Wesley. 1899.
Lee, Sidney. Dictionary of National Biography. New York, 1897.
Lloyd, F. E. J. American Church Directory. Uniontown, Pa., 1905.
Osborn, G. Articles of Wesleyan Bibliography; or a Record of Methodist Literature. London, 1869.
Townsend, William John, Workman, H. B. and Eayrs, George. A New History of Methodism. London, 1909.

Secondary Works

Abbey, C. J. The English Church in the 18th Century. London, 1878. 2 vols.
Banfield, Frank. John Wesley. Boston, 1900.
Barr, Josiah Henry. Early Methodists under Persecution. New York, 1916.
Bogue, David and Bennett, James. History of Dissenters from the Restoration. London, 1809. 4 vols.
Burckhardt, J. G. Vollständige Geschichte der Methodisten in England aus glaubwürdigen Quellen. Nürnberg, 1895.
Cadman, S. Parkes. The Three Religious Leaders of Oxford. . . . New York, 1916.
Corrie, G. E. Homilies of the Church of England. Cambridge, 1850.
Davenport, F. M. Primitive Traits in Religious Revivals. New York, 1905.
Davis, C. H. The English Church Canons of 1604. . . . London, 1869.
Faulkner, John Alfred. The Methodists. New York, 1903.
Faulkner, John Alfred. Wesley as a Churchman. American Society of Church History. Papers, 1897. Vol. viii, pp. 163-178.
Fitchett, W. H. Wesley and His Century. London, 1906.
Gee and Hardy. Documents Illustrative of English Church History. London, 1914.
Giddings, Franklin H. Readings in Descriptive and Historical Sociology. New York, 1911.
Ivimey, Joseph. History of English Baptists. London, 1814. Vols. ii and iii.
Jacoby, L. S. Geschichte des Methodismus, seiner Entstehung und Ausbreitung. Bremen, 1870. 2 vols.

Lecky, W. E. H. History of England in the 18th Century. 1878-1890. 6 vols.
Leger, Augustine. La Jeunesse de Wesley. Paris, 1910.
Leliévre, M. J. Wesley, sa Vie et son Ouvre. Paris, 1868.
(Anon.) Life and Times of Selina, Countess of Huntingdon by a Member of the House of Shirley and Hastings. London, 1839-40. 2 vols.
McGiffert, A. C. Origin of High-Church Episcopacy. In The American Journal of Theology. 1902. Pp. 417-438.
Mason, A. J. The Church of England and the Episcopacy. Cambridge, 1914.
North, E. M. Early Methodist Philanthropy. New York, 1914.
Overton, John Henry. The Church in England. London, 1897. 2 vols.
Overton, John Henry. Church of England from 1714-1800. (S.L.) 1906.
Overton, John Henry. The English Church in the 19th Century. London, 1894.
Overton, John Henry. The Evangelical Revival in the 18th Century. London, 1886.
Overton, John Henry. John Wesley. New York, 1891.
Perry, Cannon. History of the Church of England. London, 1861. 3 vols.
Simon, J. S. The Revival of Religion in England in the 18th Century. London, 1911.
Smith, George. History of Wesleyan Methodism. London, 1858-61. 3 vols.
Stevens, Abel. The History of the Movement of the 18th Century Called Methodism. New York, 1858. 4 vols.
Stevens, Abel. Life and Times of Nathan Bangs. New York, 1863.
Stevens, Abel. Memorials of the Early Progress of Methodism. Boston, 1852.
Telford, John. History of Lay Preaching in the Christian Church. London, 1897.
Tyerman, Luke. Life and Times of John Wesley. New York, 1870. 3 vols.
Tyerman, Luke. Life, Letters and Literary Labors of John William Fletcher. New York, 1883.
Waddington, John. Congregational History. London, 1876.
Walcott, Mackenzie E. C. The Constitutions and Canons Ecclesiastical of the Church of England. London, 1874.
Wesleyan Studies by Various Writers. With unpublished letters, diaries and journals. London, 1903.
Workman, Herbert Brook. Methodism. Cambridge, 1912.

PRIMARY WORKS

Atmore, Charles. Methodist Memorial. Bristol, 1801.
Benham, D. Memoirs of J. Hutton. London, 1856.
Butler, Joseph. The Analogy of Religion. . . . London, 1736.
Clarke, Adam. Memoires of Wesley Family. . . . New York, 1824.
Cooke, Joseph. Methodism Condemned. . . . Two Sermons on Justification by Faith and the Witness of the Spirit. Rochdale, 1807.
Crowther, Jonothan. A True and Complete Portraiture of Methodism or the History of the Wesleyan Methodists. . . . New York, 1813.
(Foster, J. K.) Life and Times of Selina, Countess of Huntingdon. London, 1844. 2 vols.
Gillies, John. Memoirs of George Whitefield. New Haven, 1834.
Green, Thomas. A Dissertation on Enthusiasm. . . . London, 1855.
Hampson, John. Memoirs of the Late John Wesley. . . . Sunderland, 1791. 3 vols.
Jackson, Thomas. The Centenary of Wesleyan Methodism. 1839.
Jackson, Thomas. John Wesley's Prose Works. . . . Bristol, 1771-74. 32 vols.
Jackson, Thomas. Life of the Rev. Charles Wesley, M.A. New York, 1844.
Law, William. Works. London, 1892. 9 vols.
Meacham, A. G. A Compendious History of the Rise and Progress of the Methodist Church. 1835.

Moore, Rev. Henry. Life of the Rev. John Wesley. New York, 1824. 2 vols.
Myles, William. A Chronological History of the People Called Methodists. London, 1813.
Nightingale, J. . . . View of the Rise, Progress, etc., of the Wesleyan Methodists. London, 1807.
Outram, Edmund. Sermons and Extracts. Cambridge, 1809.
Porteus, Beilby. A Review of the Life and Character of Archbishop Secker. New York, 1773.
Porteus, Beilby. Works. London, 1811. 6 vols.
Roberts, W. Memoirs of Hannah More. 1836.
Southey, Robert. The Life of Wesley; and the Rise and Progress of Methodism. . . . New York, 1847. 2 vols. 2nd American ed.
Stevens, Abel. The Centenary of American Methodism. New York, 1866.
Taylor, John. The Scripture-Doctrine of Original Sin Proposed to Free and Candid Examination to which is Added a Supplement. London, 1750.
Thompson, H. Life of Hannah More. London, 1836. 4 vols.
Webb, John. An Appeal to the Honest and Sincere Hearted Among the People Called Methodists and Quakers. London, 1753.
Wesley, Charles. Journal. London, 1849. 2 vols.
Wesley, Charles. The Journal of the Rev. Charles Wesley. New York, 1909.
Wesley, Charles. Life. New York, 1820. 2 vols.
Whitefield, George. Collection of Letters. London, 1772. 3 vols.
Whitefield, George. Journal. London, 1739-41. 7 vols.
Whitefield, George. Whitefield's Journals. To which is Prefixed his "Short Account" and "Further Account." London, 1905.
Whitehead, John. Life of John Wesley to which is Prefixed Some Account of His Ancestors together with the Life of Charles Wesley. Dublin, 1805.
Wilberforce, Samuel. History of the Protestant Episcopal Church in America. London, 1844.
Wilberforce, William. A View of the Prevailing Religious System. 1797.
Wilson, (Bishop) Maxims of Piety and Christianity. 1781.
Wilson, Walter. History and Antiquities of Dissenting Churches. 1804-14. 4 vols.
Woodward, Dr. Josiah. Account of the Rise and Progress of the Religious Societies in the City of London. . . . London, 1698.

PERIODICALS

American Society of Church History. Papers. Vols. 7 and 8. New York, 1895-1897.
The Arminian Magazine. London, 1779- . The name later changed to Methodist Magazine.
Bennett, John. Minutes of the Conferences of 1744, 1745, 1747, and 1748. In the Publications of the Wesleyan Historical Society for 1896.
Gentlemen's Magazine. London, 1747-1752.
Methodist Magazine. 1778-1821. Begun as Arminian Magazine, 1778-91, continued as the Wesleyan Magazine, 1822-
Minutes of the Annual Conferences of the Methodist Episcopal Church. New York, 1840. Vol. i. 1773-1828.
Minutes of the Methodist Conferences. London, 1812. Vol. i, 1744-98. 1813. Vol. ii, 1799-1806.
Minutes of Methodist Conferences. Philadelphia, 1795.
Minutes of Several Conversations between the Rev. Mr. Wesley and Others. 1744-1789. Works. Vol. v, pp. 211-239.
Minutes of Several Conversations between the Rev. Mr. Wesley and Chas. Wesley and Others. From the Year 1744 to the Year 1780. London, S.D.
Minutes of Some Late Conversations between the Rev. Messrs. Wesley and Others. 1744-1747 inclusive. Works. Vol. v, pp. 194-211.
Watchman's Lantern. Being a Series of Papers Intended to Throw Light on the Proceedings of the Wesleyan Methodist Conference, and its

Representatives. Liverpool, 1835. Contains the Constitution of 1795 and 1797.
Wesleyan Historical Society. Proceedings. London, 1897- . Printed for the Society. 9 vols.
Wesleyan Historical Society. Publications. London, 1897.

PAMPHLETS

(Anon.) Address to the Members and Friends of the Methodist Society in Newcastle. S. L. 1792.
(Anon). An Apology for the Methodists of the New Connection. S. L. 1815.
Bate, James. Methodism Displayed. . . . London, 1739.
(Beard, John Reilly.) Rise, Progress and Present Influence of Methodism. London, 1831.
Beilby, Lord Bishop of Chester. A Letter to the Clergy of the Diocese of Chester. 1781.
Benson, Joseph. A Defense of the Methodists in Five Letters Addressed to Rev. Dr. Tatham. London, 1794. 3rd ed.
(Berridge, J.) Justification by Faith Alone. London, 1758.
Bickerstaff, Isaac. The Hypocrite, a Comedy. Philadelphia, 1826. Published first in England in 1768.
(Lavington, George.) The Bishop of Exeter's Answer to Mr. John Wesley's Later Letter to his Lordship. London, 1752.
Boehm, Anthony William. The Doctrine of Justification Set Forth in a Sermon. . . . London, 1714.
Bradburn, Samuel. Methodism Set Forth and Defended in a Sermon. . . . Bristol, 1792.
Bradburn, Samuel. The Question, Are Methodists Dissenters? S. L. 1792.
Collins, B. B. An Address to the Higher Ranks of People in the Parish of St. Mary, Hull. Leeds, 1779. 3rd ed.
Coke, Thomas. An Address to the Inhabitants of Birstal and Adjacent Villages. Leeds, 1782.
Coke, Thomas. A Letter to the Author of Strictures on Dr. Coke's Sermon. . . . London, 1786.
Coke, Thomas. The Substance of a Sermon Preached at Baltimore before the General Conference of the Methodist Episcopal Church at the Ordination of the Rev. Francis Asbury to the Office of a Superintendent. London, 1785.
Coventry, Henry. Philemon and Hydaspes. London, 1786.
Crowther, Jonothan. The Crisis of Methodism. . . . Bristol, 1795.
Crowther, Jonothan. Christian Order: or, Liberty without Anarchy. . . . Bristol, 1796.
(Anon.) Deism Genuine anti-Methodism or, The Present Increase of Deism. . . . by a Woman. S. L. 1751.
(Anon.) The Doctrinal of Original Sin. Extracted from a Late Author. London, 1784.
Downes, John. Methodism Examined and Exposed. . . . London, 1759.
(Anon.) An Essay on the Character of Methodism. Cambridge, 1781.
Evan, Caleb. A Letter to the Rev. Mr. John Wesley; Occasioned by his Calm Address to the American Colonies. London, 1775.
(Evans, Theophilus.) The History of Enthusiasm from the Reformation to the Present Time. London, 1757.
Fletcher, John William. An Appeal to the Matter of Fact and Common Sense. Or a Rational Demonstration of Man's Lost Estate. . . . Philadelphia, 1794.
Fletcher, John William. Checks to Antinomianism in a Series of Letters to the Rev. Mr. Shirley and Mr. Hill. New York, 1771-1774. 2 vols.
Fletcher, J. W. Vindication of . . . Wesley's "Calm Address to our American Colonies" in Some Letters to Caleb Evans. . . . London, S.D.
Fletcher, John William. A Vindication of Mr. Wesley's Last Minutes . . . as a Dreadful Heresy. Bristol, 1771.

FROM THE CHURCH OF ENGLAND 179

Free, John. Controversy with the People Called Methodists. . . . London, 1760.
Free, John. Rules for the Discovery of False Prophets. . . . London, 1759.
Free, John. Sermon Preached before the University at St. Mary's in Oxford. . . . London, 1758.
Free, John. Whole Speech. . . . Delivered to the Rev. Clergy of the Great City of London. London, (1759).
Gill, John. The Doctrine of Predestination Stated . . . ; in Opposition to Mr. Wesley's Predestination Calmly Considered. . . . London, 1752.
Gibson, Edmund. The Bishop of London's Pastoral Letter to the People of his Diocese . . . by Way of Caution against Lukewarmness on the One Hand, and Enthusiasm on the Other. London, 1739.
Gibson, Edmund. Caution against Enthusiasm, being the Second Part of the Bishop of London's 4th Pastoral Letter. London, 1801.
(Gibson, Edmund.) An Earnest Appeal to the Public. . . . London, 1739.
(Gibson, Edmund.) Observations upon the Conduct and Behaviour of a Certain Sect Usually Distinguished by the Name of Methodists. London, 1744.
(Green, John.) The Principles of a Methodist Farther Considered in a Letter to Rev. Mr. George Whitefield. Cambridge, 1761.
(Grey, Zachary.) A Serious Address to Lay-Methodists to Beware of the False Pretences of their Teachers with an Appendix . . . an Account of the Bloody Effects of Enthusiasm. London, 1745.
Henchman, Nathaniel. A Letter from N—— H—— to Rev. Stephen Chase, of —— Giving his Reasons for Declining to Admit the Rev. George Whitefield into his Pulpit. Boston, 1745.
Hill, Rowland. A Full Answer to the Rev. J. Wesley's Remarks. Bristol, 1777.
(Hill, Rowland.) A review of All the Doctrines Taught by the Rev. Mr. John Wesley . . . and a Farrago. London, 1772.
Kilham, Alexander. Methodist Monitor . . . Containing Appendix of Trial. (1796.) Vol. I.
Kirby, John. The Impostor Detected or; the Counterfeit Saint Turned Inside Out. London, 1750.
Lavington, Bishop George. Enthusiasm of Methodists and Papists Compared. London, 1820. This is a reprint of an earlier edition. 493 pages.
Lefroy, Christopher Edward. Are these Things So, or, Some Quotations and Remarks in Defense of What the World Calls Methodism. London, 1809.
(Anon.) A Letter from a Clergyman to One of His Parishioners Who was Inclined to Turn Methodist. London, 1753.
London, Bishop of. A Caution against Enthusiasm. Being a 2nd Part of the Late . . . Fourth Pastoral Letter. London, 1751.
(Longridge, M.) A Conciliatory Essay, Addressed to the Methodists, in General. Sunderland, 1795.
Martin, John. Imposture Detected, or Thoughts on a Pretended Prophet and on the Prevalence of His Impositions. London, 1787.
Mason, William. Methodism, Displayed and Enthusiasm Detected. S.L. and S.D.
(M. B.) Some General Remarks on a Late Pamphlet Entitled, the Enthusiasm of the Methodists and Papists Compared in a Letter to a Gentleman. S.L. Very old.
(Anon.) The Methodist and Mimick. A Tale . . . Inscribed to Samuel Foot, Esq. London. 1767.
(Anon.) The Methodists Dissected; or an Impartial Inquiry into the Conduct of those Arch Methodists G. W. and C. W. Oxford, S.D.
(Anon.) Methodism and Popery Dissected and Compared and the Doctrine of Both Proven to be of Pagan Origin. London, 1779.
Moore, Henry. A Reply to a Pamphlet Entitled "Considerations on a Separation of the Methodists from the Established Church." Bristol, 1794.

Morgan, J. M. Letter to the Bishop of London. London, 1830.
Morgan, Thomas. Nature and Consequences of Enthusiasm. London, 1719.
(Anon.) Observations and Remarks on Mr. Seagrave's Conduct and Writings. . . . London, 1739.
(Paul and Silas.) An Earnest Address to the Preachers Assembled in Conference. . . . S.L. 1795.
Perronet, Vincent. A Third Letter to the Author of a Piece, Entitled, the Enthusiasm of Methodists and Papists Compared. London, 1752.
(Anon.) A Plain Address to the Followers and Favorers of the Methodists. London, S.D. and S.L.
Priestly, Joseph. Original Letters by Rev. John Wesley and His Friends. . . . Birmingham, 1791.
(　　) Primitive Methodism Defended. Address from Trustees of Broadmead and Guinea Street Chapels in Bristol. . . . Bristol, 1795.
(Anon.) The Principles and Practices of the Methodists Considered in Some Letters to the Leaders of that Sect. The First Address to Rev. Mr. [Berridge] wherein are Some Remarks on his Two Letters to a Clergyman in Nottinghamshire, Lately Published. London, 1761.
(Anon.) The Question, Whether it be Right to Turn Methodist Considered in a Dialogue between Two Members of the Church of England. London, 1745.
Rhodes, Benjamin. The Point Stated . . . and a Short Plan of Reconciliation Proposed. . . . Birmingham, 1795.
Rimus, Henry. A Candid Narrative of the Rise and Progress of the Herrenhuters Commonly Called Moravians. . . . London, 1753.
Roe, Samuel. Enthusiasm Detected, Defeated . . . Cambridge, 1768.
(Anon.) A Serious and Affectionate Address to the Members of the Church of England on their Falling Away from her Articles and Homilies. London, 1757.
(Shaver, The) Priestcraft Defended. A Sermon Occasioned by the Expulsion of Six Young Gentlemen from Oxford for Praying, Reading and Expounding Scriptures. London, 1768.
(　　) A Short Account of the Late Rev. J. Wesley, A.M., During the Last Two Weeks of His Life Collected from Persons who Attended Him During that Time. London, 1791.
Simpson, David. The Happiness of Dying in the Lord; with an Apology for the Methodists. . . . Manchester, 1784.
Smith, Haddon. Methodistical Deceit: a Sermon Preached in the Parish Church of St. Matthew . . . Middlesex on the 29th of April, 1770. London, 1770.
Snell, John. The Substance of a Sermon Preached the 20th Day of August 1775 in the Parish of North-Tawton. London, (1776).
Stebbing, Henry. Caution against Religious Delusion. S.L. 1739.
Sutcliffe, Joseph. Christian Liberty: or Consideration on the Propriety of the Methodists having the Lord's Supper in their own Chapels. Bristol, 1795.
Taylor, Thomas. A Defense of the Methodists who do not Attend the National Church, but Avail Themselves of Liberty of Conscience. Liverpool, 1792.
(Tillotson, John.)—Archbishop of Canterbury. A Persuasive to Frequent Communion. S.L. and S.D.
Toplady, A. M. More Work for Mr. John Wesley; or a Vindication of the Decrees and Providence of God. . . . London, 1772.
Toplady, Augustus. An Old Fox Tarr'd and Feathered; Occasioned by what is Called Mr. Wesley's Calm Address. . . . London, 1775.
Tottie, John. Two Charges to the Clergy of the Diocese of Worcester in the Years 1763-1766. Oxford, 1766.
(Anon.) The True Spirit of the Methodists and their Allies. . . . London, 1740.

Trustees of Broadmead Chapel, Bristol. Primitive Methodism Defended in an Address from the Trustees of Broadmead and Guinea Chapels in Bristol. Bristol, (1795).
Tucker, Josiah. Brief History of the Principles of Methodism. . . . Oxford, 1742.
Tucker, Josiah. A Complete Account of the Conduct of the Eminent Enthusiast, Mr. Whitefield. London, 1739.
(Tucker, Josiah.) Genuine and Secret Memoirs Relating to the Life and Adventures of that Arch-Methodist George Whitefield. Oxford, 1742.
Wainewright, Latham. Observations on the Doctrine, Discipline and Manners of the Wesleyan Methodists and also of the Evangelical Party. . . . London, 1818.
Warburton, William. Tracts by ———. London, 1789.
Warren, Samuel. Chronicles of Methodism. . . . London, 1827. Vol. i.
Watts, Isaac. An Humble Attempt toward the Revival of Practical Religion among Christians. . . . London, 1731.
Wesley, Charles. Facsimile Ms. Letter to Dr. Chandler. London, April, 28, 1785.
(Wesleyan Methodist). Methodist Error, or Friendly Christian Advice. Trenton, N. J., 1819.
Whitefield, Rev. George. Expostulatory Letter, Addressed to Nicholas Lewis, Count Zinzendorff, and Lord . . . London, 1756.
Whitefield, George. A Continuation of the Rev. Mr. Whitefield's Journal during the Time he was Detained in England by the Embargo. London, 1739.
Whitefield, Rev. George. Letter to the Rev. Dr. Durell Occasioned by a Late Expulsion of Students from Edmund Hall. . . . London, 1768.
Whitefield, Rev. George. Letter to the President and Professors, Tutors and Hebrew Instructor of Harvard College . . . in Answer to a Testimony Published by them against the Rev. George Whitefield and his Conduct. Boston, 1745.
Whitefield, Rev. George. Letter to Thomas Church . . . in Answer to his Serious Letter to George Whitefield. London, 1744.
Whitefield, George. Observations on Some Fatal Mistakes in a Book. . . . The Doctrine of Grace . . . by Dr. William Warburton, Lord Bishop of Gloucester. . . . London, 1763.
Whitefield, George. The Rev. Mr. Whitefield's Answer, to the Bishop of London's Last Pastoral Letter. London, 1739. 2nd ed.
Whitefield, George. Select Collections of Letters. . . . Written Intimate Friends and Persons of Distinction. . . . London, 1772. 3 vols.
Whitefield, George. Sermons. Bound with Memoirs of George Whitefield, edited by John Gillies. q.v.
Whitefield, George. The Testimony of the President, Professors . . . of Harvard College against . . . and his Conduct. Boston, 1744.
Whitehead, John. Discourse at the Funeral of John Wesley. S.L. 1845.
(Wills). Remarks on Methodism. London, 1813.

Works of John Wesley

Eayrs, George. Letters of John Wesley. New York, 1915.
Emory, John. Works of John Wesley. New York, 1831. Complete in 7 vols. The following writings of Wesley were taken from this publication for use in this thesis:
An Address to the Clergy. Athlone, 1756. Vol. vi, pp. 217-236.
Advice to the People Called Methodists. S.L., 1745. Vol. v, pp. 249-254.
Advice to the People Called Methodists, with Regard to Dress. S.L. and S.D. Vol. vi, pp. 545-553.
An Answer to an Important Question. 1787. Vol. vii, pp. 317-319.
An Answer to Mr. Rowland Hill's Tract Entitled "Imposture Detected." London, 1777. Vol. vi, pp. 193-199.

The Case of the Birstal House. London, 1788. Vol. vii, pp. 326-329.
The Case of the Dewsbury House. Bristol, 1789. Vol. vii, pp. 329-330.
The Character of the Methodist. . . . Bristol, 1743. Vol. v, pp. 240-245.
A Collection of Forms of Prayer for Every Day in the Week. 1733. Vol. vi, pp. 377-426.
Directions Concerning Pronunciation and Gesture. Vol. vii, pp. 487-493.
Directions Given to the Band Societies. 1744. Vol. v, pp. 193-194.
Directions to the Stewards of the Methodist Society in London. 1747. Vol. vii, pp. 486-487.
The Doctrine of Original Sin. Bristol, 1757. Vol. v, pp. 492-669.
An Estimate of the Manners of the Present Times. 1782. vol. vi, pp. 347-352
An Extract from: A Short View of the Difference between the Moravian Brethren and the Rev. Mr. John and Charles Wesley. Vol. vi, pp. 22-24.
An Extract of a Letter to the Rev. Mr. Law. London, 1756. Vol. v, pp. 669-699.
Farther Thoughts on Separation from the Church. London, 1789. Vol. vii, pp. 325-326.
A Letter to a Clergyman. Bristol, 1766. Vol. v, pp. 349-352.
A Letter to a Friend. 1761. Vol. vii, p. 299.
A Letter to a Friend Concerning Tea. Newington, 1748. Vol. vi, pp. 567-575.
A Letter to the Rev. Mr. Baily . . . in Answer to a Letter to a Letter. . . . London, 1750. Vol. v, pp. 407-423.
A Letter to the Rev. Conyers Middleton, Occasioned by his Late Free Inquiry, Bristol, 1749. Vol. v, pp. 705-761.
A Letter to the Rev. Mr. Downes. London, 1759. Vol. v, pp. 428-437.
A Letter to the Rev. Mr. Fleury. Dublin, 1771. Vol. v, pp. 484-491.
A Letter to the Rev. Dr. Free. Bristol, 1758. Vol. v, pp. 352-354.
A Letter to the Rev. Mr. Horne: Occasioned by his Sermon Preached before the University of Oxford. London, 1762. Vol. v, pp. 438-442.
A Letter to the Rev. John Taylor. Hartlepool, 1759. Vol. v, p. 669.
A Letter to the Rt. Rev. the Lord Bishop of London; Occasioned by his Lordship's Late Charge to his Clergy. London, 1747. Vol. v, pp. 339-349.
A Letter to Mr. T. H., alias Philodemos, alias Somebody. . . . Vol. vii, pp. 400-403.
A Letter to the Rev. Mr. Potter. London, 1758. Vol. v, pp. 423-427.
A Letter to the Rev. Mr. Toogood, of Exeter; Occasioned by his "Dissent from the Church of England Fully Justified." Bristol, 1758. Vol. vi, pp. 231-234.
The Nature, Design, and General Rules of the United Societies. . . . 1743. Vol. v, pp. 190-192.
The Principles of a Methodist Occasioned by a Late Pamphlet, entitled "A Brief History of the Principles of Methodism." Vol. v, pp. 251-264.
The Principles of a Methodist Farther Explained Occasioned by the Rev. Mr. Church's Second Letter to Mr. Wesley. London, 1746. Vol. v, pp. 292-328.
To the Printer of the Dublin Chronicle. Londonderry, June 2, 1789. Vol. vii, pp. 222-224.
Reasons Against Separation from the Church of England. 1758. Vol. vii, pp. 293-298.
Rules of the Band Societies. 1738. Vol. v, pp. 192-193.
Of Separation from the Church. 1785. Vol. vii, pp. 313-315.
A Second Letter to the Lord Bishop of Exeter, in Answer to his Lordship's Later Letter. London, 1752. Vol. v, pp. 405-407.

A Short Account of the Life and Death of the Rev. John Fletcher. 1786. Vol. vi, pp. 427-483.
A Short Address to the Inhabitants of Ireland Occasioned by Some Late Occurrences. Dublin, 1749. Vol. v, p. 480-484.
A Short History of Methodism. (1764.) Vol. v, pp. 246-248.
Some Thoughts upon an Important Question. 1781. Vol. vii, p. 306.
Specimen of the Divinity and Philosophy of the Highly-Illuminated Jacob Behmen. S.L. and S.D. Vol. v, pp. 703-705.
Thoughts on the Consecration of Churches and Burial Grounds. Dumfries, 1788. Vol. vi, pp. 236-237.
Thoughts on Separation from the Church. Bristol, 1788. Vol. vii, p. 319.
Thoughts Upon a Late Phenomenon. Nottingham, 1788. Vol. vii, pp. 319-321.
A Word to Whom it May Concern. London, 1790. Vol. vii, p. 332.
Wesley, John. An Answer to the Rev. Mr. Churche's Remarks on the Rev. John Wesley's Journal, in a Letter to that Gentleman. Bristol, 1745.
Wesley, John. A Blow at the Root; or Christ Stabbed in the House of His Friends. Bristol, 1762. 2nd ed.
Wesley, John. Calm Address to Our American Colonies. Dublin, 1775.
Wesley, John. A Calm Address to Our American Colonies. A new edition, corrected and enlarged. London, 1775.
The Christian Sacrament and Sacrifice. Extracted from a late author by . . . London, 1794.
A Compassionate Address to the Inhabitants of Ireland. Belfast, 1778.
Deed of Declaration. (In Appendix B, p. 551, Townsend's History of Methodism q.v.)
Duty of Constant Communion. New York, 1788.
An Earnest Appeal to Men of Reason and Religion. Newcastle on Tyne, 1743.
(Wesley, John.) An Earnest Invitation to the Friends of the Established Church to Join . . . in Setting apart One Hour of Every Week, for Prayer and Supplication, during the Present Troublous Times. London, 1779.
Wesley, John. An Extract of Mr. Richard Baxter's Aphorisms of Justification. London, 1784.
A Farther Appeal to Men of Reason and Religion. London, 1745.
Free Thoughts on the Present State of Affairs. In a Letter to a Friend. London, 1770.
The Heart of John Wesley's Journal, with an Introduction by Hugh Price Hughes. . . . New York, 1903.
(Wesley, John and Charles.) Hymns for the Nativity of our Lord. Bristol, 1750.
Wesley, John and Charles. Hymns for the Year 1756. Bristol, 1756.
Wesley, John. The Journal of the Rev. John Wesley, London, 1907. 4 vols.
The Journal of the Rev. John Wesley. . . . New York, 1909. Complete in 8 vols. The Best and most useful to date.
A Letter to the Author of the Craftsman. . . . London, 1745.
A Letter to the Author of Enthusiasm of Methodists and Papists Compared. London, 1749-50.
A Letter to the Bishops of London: Occasioned by His Lordship's Late Charge to his Clergy. Bristol, 1749.
Letter to Lord Bishop of Gloucester. London, 1763.
A Letter to a Person Lately Joined with the Call'd Quakers. S.L. 1748.
A Letter to the Rev. Mr. Law: Occasioned by Some of his Late Writings. London, 1756.
The Miscellanous Works of . . . New York, 1828. 3 vols.
Nicodemus: or a Treatise on the Fear of Man. Written in German by Augustus Herman Francke, Abridged by . . . London, 1798.
A Plain Account of Christian Perfection. New York, 1837.

A Plain Account of the People Called Methodists in a Letter to the Rev. Mr. Perronet. London, 1755.
Predestination Calmly Considered. London, 1797.
A Preservative against Unsettled Notions in Religion. Bristol, 1770.
Reflections Upon the Conduct of Human Life; with Reference to Learning and Knowledge. Extracted by . . . London, 1798.
The Scripture Doctrine Concerning Predestination, Election. . . . S.L. and S.D.
Scripture Doctrine of Predestination, Election and Reprobation also the Nature and Extent of the Atonement. New York, 1813.
A Second Letter to the Rev. Dr. Free. Bristol, 1758.
Sermons, Chiefly on the Spiritual Life. New York, 1871. Edited by Abel Stevens.
Sermons on Several Occasions. Devon, 1826.
Sermons on Several Occasions. New York, 1830. 2 vols.
A Short Exposition of the Ten Commandments Extracted from Bishop Hopkins by . . . London, 1799.
A Short History of Methodism. London, 1765.
Short View of the Difference Between the Moravian Brethren. London, 1745.
Some Observations on Liberty Occasioned by a Late Tract. London, 1776.
Some Remarks Upon Mr. Hill's Review of all the Doctrines Taught by Mr. John Wesley. Bristol, 1772.
Some Remarks Upon Mr. Hill's Farrago Double-Distilled. Bristol, 1773.
The Sunday Service of the Methodists in the United States of America with Other Occasional Services. London, 1790.
Thoughts Upon Necessity. London, 1775.
A Treatise on Christian Prudence. Extracted from Mr. Morrs by . . . London, 1784. 4th ed.
A Word in Season: or Advice to an Englishman. S.L. and S.D. 7th ed.
The Works of John Wesley. New York, 1826. 10 vols.

VITA

ROBERT LEONARD TUCKER was born in Westfield, Massachusetts, January 28, 1890. After graduating from the high school of that place in 1909, he entered Wesleyan University of Middletown, Connecticut, from which he received the degree of B.A., in 1913. In 1915 he received the degree of Master of Arts from Columbia University. In 1916 he graduated from Union Theological Seminary, of New York City after completing three years of study. It was from 1915-1918 that he was a candidate in Columbia University for the degree of Doctor of Philosophy. He is an ordained minister in the Methodist Episcopal Church.

www.ingramcontent.com/pod-product-compliance
Lightning Source LLC
Chambersburg PA
CBHW050807160426
43192CB00010B/1670